First World War
and Army of Occupation
War Diary
France, Belgium and Germany

58 DIVISION
175 Infantry Brigade
London Regiment
1/12 Battalion
19 January 1917 - 30 January 1918

WO95/3009/8

The Naval & Military Press Ltd
www.nmarchive.com
Published in association with The National Archives

Published by

The Naval & Military Press Ltd

Unit 10 Ridgewood Industrial Park,

Uckfield, East Sussex,

TN22 5QE England

Tel: +44 (0) 1825 749494

www.naval-military-press.com

www.nmarchive.com

This diary has been reprinted in facsimile from the original. Any imperfections are inevitably reproduced and the quality may fall short of modern type and cartographic standards.

© **Crown Copyright**
Images reproduced by permission of The National Archives, London, England, 2015.

Contents

Document type	Place/Title	Date From	Date To
Heading	WO95/3009/7		
Heading	War Diary 2/11th Battn Lond: Regiment From Jan 19th-1917 To Feb 26th 1917		
War Diary	Longbridge Deverill	19/01/1917	02/02/1917
War Diary	Le Souich	11/02/1917	13/02/1917
War Diary	Souastre	13/02/1917	13/02/1917
War Diary	Fonquevillers	14/02/1917	17/02/1917
War Diary	Sovastre	18/02/1917	18/02/1917
War Diary	Halloy	18/02/1917	25/02/1917
Heading	War Diary 2/11th Battn Lond Rgt		
War Diary	Halloy	27/02/1917	27/02/1917
War Diary	Gaudiempre	27/02/1917	28/02/1917
War Diary	Riviere	28/02/1917	28/02/1917
War Diary	Sub-Sector F.2	01/03/1917	05/03/1917
War Diary	Bellacourt	05/03/1917	06/03/1917
War Diary	Sub Sector D.I	07/03/1917	18/03/1917
War Diary	Bellacourt	18/03/1917	19/03/1917
War Diary	Grosville	20/03/1917	22/03/1917
War Diary	Laherliere	22/03/1917	25/03/1917
War Diary	Halloy	25/03/1917	26/03/1917
Map	Map		
Heading	War Diary 2/11th Battn London Regiment From:- March 27th-1917 To:- April 26th-1917		
War Diary	Halloy	27/03/1917	31/03/1917
War Diary	Barley	01/04/1917	02/04/1917
War Diary	Buire Au Bois	03/04/1917	05/04/1917
War Diary	Bus Les Artois	06/04/1917	08/04/1917
War Diary	Miramont	09/04/1917	09/04/1917
War Diary	Achiet Le Petit	10/04/1917	26/04/1917
Miscellaneous	Scheme for The defence Of Subsector D1		
Heading	War Diary 2/XI Battn London Regt. Volume 4 From April 27th 1917 To May 26-1917		
War Diary	Achiet Le Petit	27/04/1917	04/05/1917
War Diary	57c NW 1/20000 C 30 A 28	05/05/1917	08/05/1917
War Diary	C 30.A 28	09/05/1917	09/05/1917
War Diary	57c NW 1/20000 C 20 A 28	09/05/1917	11/05/1917
War Diary	I.Y.C.86	12/05/1917	12/05/1917
War Diary	Favreuil	13/05/1917	15/05/1917
War Diary	Bihucourt	15/05/1917	21/05/1917
War Diary	Bullecourt Right Sector	21/05/1917	25/05/1917
War Diary	C 30 A Central	26/05/1917	26/05/1917
Heading	War Diary 2/XI Battn London Regt Volume 5 From 27th To 30th June		
War Diary	Mory	27/05/1917	04/06/1917
War Diary	Bullecourt Rt Front Sub-Sector	05/06/1917	15/06/1917
War Diary	Mory	15/06/1917	16/06/1917
War Diary	St Leger	16/06/1917	17/06/1917
War Diary	Mory	18/06/1917	24/06/1917
War Diary	Logeast Wood	25/06/1917	30/06/1917

Type	Description	Start	End
Heading	War Diary 2/XIth Battn London Regiment Volume VI From July 1st 1917 To July 31st 1917		
War Diary	Logeast Wood	01/07/1917	05/07/1917
War Diary	Bancourt	06/07/1917	06/07/1917
War Diary	Bertincourt	07/07/1917	08/07/1917
War Diary	Havrincourt Sector	09/07/1917	16/07/1917
War Diary	Havrin Court Left Front Sub Sector	16/07/1917	27/07/1917
War Diary	Warlus	28/07/1917	31/07/1917
Heading	War Diary 2/11 Battn London Regt From 1st August 1917 To 31st August 1917 Volume 1		
War Diary	Warlus	01/08/1917	25/08/1917
War Diary	Brake Camp	26/08/1917	27/08/1917
War Diary	Raigesburg Camp	28/08/1917	28/08/1917
War Diary	Yser Canal Bank	29/08/1917	31/08/1917
Heading	War Diary 2nd/XIth Bn London Regt. From 1st September 1917 To 30th September 1917		
War Diary	Yser Canal	01/09/1917	01/09/1917
War Diary	St Julien	02/09/1917	06/09/1917
War Diary	Yser Canal	06/09/1917	06/09/1917
War Diary	Dembre Camp	07/09/1917	11/09/1917
War Diary	Brake Camp	12/09/1917	20/09/1917
War Diary	California Drive Ypres Salient	21/09/1917	21/09/1917
War Diary	Ypres Salient	22/09/1917	27/09/1917
War Diary	Dambre Camp	28/09/1917	30/09/1917
Map	Map		
Heading	War Diary-Volume I Of 11th Bn London Regt		
War Diary	Brake Camp	01/10/1917	02/10/1917
War Diary	Recques	03/10/1917	21/10/1917
War Diary	Road Camp	22/10/1917	30/10/1917
War Diary	Siege Camp	31/10/1917	31/10/1917
Heading	War Diary 2/XIth Bn. London Regt From 1st November 1917 To 31st November 1917		
War Diary	Yser Canal Bank	01/11/1917	02/11/1917
War Diary	Kempton Park	03/11/1917	04/11/1917
War Diary	Poelcappelle	05/11/1917	06/11/1917
War Diary	Siege Camp	07/11/1917	14/11/1917
War Diary	Proven	15/11/1917	27/11/1917
War Diary	Seninghem	28/11/1917	30/11/1917
Miscellaneous	Headquarters 58th Division.		
Heading	War Diary 2/11 London Regt From Dec 1st 1917 31st 1917		
War Diary	Seninghem	01/12/1917	06/12/1917
War Diary	Siege Camp	07/12/1917	08/12/1917
War Diary	Left Sub Sector Poelcapel Sector	09/12/1917	11/12/1917
War Diary	Left Subsector Support Position	12/12/1917	14/12/1917
War Diary	Left Subsector Forward Position	15/12/1917	16/12/1917
War Diary	Bridge Camp	17/12/1917	24/12/1917
War Diary	Left Subsector Poelcapelle Support	25/12/1917	31/12/1917
Heading	War Diary 2/11 London Regt From 1st Jan 1918 To 31st Jan 1918		
War Diary	Left Subsector Poelcapelle	01/01/1918	01/01/1918
War Diary	Bridge Camp	02/01/1918	07/01/1918
War Diary	Houtkerque Area E26d74	07/01/1918	21/01/1918
War Diary	Glisy & Blangy	22/01/1918	30/01/1918

WO 95/30097

SECRET

War Diary — 2/11th Battn: Lond: Regiment.

From Jany 19th 1917.
To. Feby 26th 1917.

10 sheets

Army Form C. 2118.

WAR DIARY
or
INTELLIGENCE SUMMARY.
(Erase heading not required.)

2/1/5 Batln. Coldm. Gds.

Col. M.H. Grant
Commanding

Place	Date	Hour	Summary of Events and Information	Remarks and references to Appendices
Cambridge Barracks	19/1/17	3 p.m.	Received Entraining orders and Rly. Time Table. The Battalion entrains at Warminster en route for SOUTHAMPTON and LE HAVRE on Jany 28th and 29th as under.	

Train No X173 12 Offrs 325 O.R. ½ Transport dep. WARMINSTER 10.40 am 28th
     "   X174 12   "   324 "   "   "   "   "   11.45 am 28th
     "   X175 10   "   330 "   8.20 am 29th

The "State" of the Battalion on receipt of the above order is as follows :—

Trained Men   634
13th Week Recruits   177
  9th   "   109
  8th   "   55
                975

In addition there are on strength 38 O.R. who are medically or professionally unfit to proceed overseas.

There are 31 Officers on strength — Above 3 still required to complete establishment.

(Battalion Captains)

Army Form C. 2118.

WAR DIARY
(2)
INTELLIGENCE SUMMARY.
(Erase heading not required.)

7/11th Batt: Lincoln Regt.

Instructions regarding War Diaries and Intelligence Summaries are contained in F.S. Regs., Part II. and the Staff Manual respectively. Title pages will be prepared in manuscript.

Places	Date	Hour	Summary of Events and Information	Remarks and references to Appendices
Longbridge Deverill	27/1/17	8.0 a.m.	Instructions received through HQ 17th Inf Bde. that troop trains for 27.1.17 and following days are cancelled pending receipt of further instructions.	B.B.Willcox Capt/Adj
Longbridge Deverill	29/1/17	4.5 p.m.	Telegram from SEARAIL received through HQ 17th Inf Bde to the effect that movements are postponed for 72 hours. The Battalion will therefore move on Jany 31st and Feby 1st 1917.	B.B.Willcox Capt/Adj
	30/1/17	12.45 p.m.	Verbal instructions received from O/C Rear Party at HQ 52nd (Res) Divn HQ. that move is further postponed. Amended instructions to be issued later.	B.B.Willcox Capt/Adj
Longbridge Deverill	1/2/17	11.50 a.m.	Instructions received by wire from Bde HQ. that move will take place on Feb 3rd and 4th.	B.B.Willcox Capt/Adj
Longbridge Deverill	2/2/17	12.15 p.m.	Move postponed one day and will be carried out on Feby 4th and 5th unless contrary Orders are issued.	B.B.Willcox Capt/Adj

Army Form C. 2118.

WAR DIARY
or
INTELLIGENCE SUMMARY.
(Erase heading not required.)

2/11th Battn London Regt (3)

Place	Date	Hour	Summary of Events and Information	Remarks and references to Appendices
LE SOUICH FRANCE.	1/2/17	2.40 am.	The Battalion left LONGBRIDGE DEVERILL on Feby 4th and 5th in two parties. Party No.1 under Lt.Col. N.H.GRANT, consisted of 23 Officers: 647 other ranks and the whole of the Battalion transport. [Feby 4th]	
			Feby 5th – left WARMINSTER 8.5 and 9.20 am. left SOUTHAMPTON 6.30 pm. (S.S. ARCHIMEDES)	
			Feby 6th – Disembarked HAVRE 8.30 am. Marched to No.1. REST CAMP 2. p.m.	
			July 6th left HAVRE REST CAMP 7.15 am. Entrained HAVRE 2.15 p.m.	
			July 7th Arrived FRÉVENT 3.45 p.m. Marched to LE SOUICH arriving at 9.20 p.m. Went into billets.	
			Casualties en route 1 man admitted to No 2 Gen: Hospital HAVRE (sick) 3 men left at REST CAMP HAVRE for several parts – suffering from chills.	O.B.Williams Captain

Army Form C. 2118.

2/1st Bn Rvd Rgt

WAR DIARY
or
~~INTELLIGENCE SUMMARY.~~
(Erase heading not required.)

(4)

Place	Date	Hour	Summary of Events and Information	Remarks and references to Appendices
LE SOUICH	10/2/17	3 pm	Party No 2 under Major W.F.J. SYMONDS consisting of 5 Officers 296 O.R.	
	Feb 5th		Left WARMINSTER 7.5 am.	
			Embarked SOUTHAMPTON 4.30 p.m. (S.S. MONA'S QUEEN)	
			During the passage an enemy submarine discharged a torpedo at the vessel but missed	
			The submarine collided with the MONA'S QUEEN rudder bow and is reported to have been sunk.	B.B.Withers Capt + Adj
	Feb 6th		Disembarked at LE HAVRE 7.0 am.	
			Marched to No 1 REST CAMP. 11.0 am	
	Feb 7th		Left REST CAMP in two parties: at (a) 6.30 am (b) 11 a.m.	
			(a) under Capt P.R. MANN (4 Off 200 O.R.) (b) under Major W.F.J.SYMONDS (1 Off 97 OR)	
			Entrained LE HAVRE 11.15 am. Entrained LE HAVRE 1 p.m.	
	Feb 8th		Arrived FREVENT 7.0 pm Arrived AUXI-LE-CHATEAU 7. pm	
			Proceeded to LE SOUICH Proceeded to LE SOUICH	
			by route march and by motor-lorry and	
			arrived at 10.30 pm arrived at 10.30 pm	

Army Form C. 2118.

WAR DIARY
or
INTELLIGENCE SUMMARY.

(5) 2/11 Batt. Royal Fus.

(Erase heading not required.)

Instructions regarding War Diaries and Intelligence Summaries are contained in F.S. Regs., Part II. and the Staff Manual respectively. Title pages will be prepared in manuscript.

Place	Date	Hour	Summary of Events and Information	Remarks and references to Appendices
LE SOUICH	11/2/17	3pm	On arrival at LE SOUICH left parties (a + b) went into Billets. Casualties en route. The party picked up two of the men left at HAVRE REST CAMP by No 1 Party and sent one the other with one man of No 2 Party to No 39 General Hospital SANVIC – LE HAVRE. The strength of the Battalion on arrival at LE SOUICH in the area of concentration was Officers 31 OR 937 and Complete transport. shewing a deficiency of :– Officers 3 OR 38. The Battalion is still in Billets at LE SOUICH on 11.2.17 the date of this entry.	O Bullieu Captain

T2134. Wt. W708–776. 500000. 4/15. Sir J. C. & 8.

Army Form C. 2118.

WAR DIARY
or
INTELLIGENCE SUMMARY.
(Erase heading not required.)

(6) 2/5 Bn. Royal Fus.

Place	Date	Hour	Summary of Events and Information	Remarks and references to Appendices
LE SOUICH	11/2/17	—	Instructions received that the Battalion will move on 13.2.17. to SOUASTRE motor-bus for attachment to 138th + 139th Bdes. The Transport to proceed to HENU.	B.R. Phillerton Captain
LE SOUICH	13/2/17	9.30 am	The Transport & Q.M. Personnel proceeded from LE SOUICH by route march to Transport Lines at HENU and Q.M. Stores at SOUASTRE	B.R. Phillerton Captain
	13/2/17	2.15 pm	The Battalion en-bused in 33 motor lorries and proceeded to SOUASTRE. Marching out state of Battn: 32 Officers 843 O.R.	
SOUASTRE	13/2/17	4.30 pm	Arrived at SOUASTRE. After an interval for dinner Companies proceeded under guides to trenches, being attached as follows:— HQ. attached to 5" Sherwood Foresters at FONQUEVILLERS Sector XI. "A" Coy " " " " " " "B" Coy " " 7th " " " X.2. "C" Coy " " 7th " " " Y.2. "D" Coy " " 4th Leicester Regt. " HANNESCAMPS.	R. Phillerton Captain E.C. Nickson Captain
FONQUEVILLERS	14/2/17	—	As above: Moderate enemy activity only.	E.C. Nickson Captain

Army Form C. 2118.

WAR DIARY
or
INTELLIGENCE SUMMARY. (7) 2/1 Batt London regt

(Erase heading not required.)

Instructions regarding War Diaries and Intelligence Summaries are contained in F. S. Regs., Part II. and the Staff Manual respectively. Title pages will be prepared in manuscript.

Place	Date	Hour	Summary of Events and Information	Remarks and references to Appendices
FONQUEVILLERS	14/2/17	7.30	2/Lt F.W. Ward accompanied a raiding party of 5th Sherwood Foresters in to the "SNOUT" and found it unoccupied by the enemy.	PR Whillons Capt & Adj
FONQUEVILLERS	15/2/17	2 pm	'A' Coy and Battn H.Q. moved to Subsector X.2. and became attached to the 7th Battn Sherwood Foresters. Platoons of 'A' & 'B' Coys took over platoon fronts in Subsector X.2. 'C' Coy took over Platoon fronts as follows: 2 Platoons with 4th Lincolns in Subsector Y.1. 2 " " 5th Leicesters " " Y.2. 'D' Coy moved to Billets at ST. AMAND. Moderate Artillery activity on both sides.	PR Whillons Capt & Adj
FONQUEVILLERS	16/2/17	9.0 am	Marked aerial activity.	PR Whillons Capt & Adj
		3.0 pm	Enemy trenches opposite Subsector X.2. were heavily bombarded during the morning.	

WAR DIARY
or
INTELLIGENCE SUMMARY. (8) 2/1th Battn. London Regt.
(Erase heading not required.)

Army Form C. 2118.

Instructions regarding War Diaries and Intelligence Summaries are contained in F. S. Regs., Part II. and the Staff Manual respectively. Title pages will be prepared in manuscript.

Place	Date	Hour	Summary of Events and Information	Remarks and references to Appendices
FONQUEVILLERS	16/2/17	5 pm	"A" & "B" Coys have taken over Company fronts in centre and left of Subsector X.2.	BB.Villers Apt-2ay
			"C" Coy moved to B'llut at ST. AMAND, being relieved in Subsector Y.1. Y.2. by "D" Coy.	
		7.0 pm	The 8th Sherwood Foresters relieve 7th Sherwood Foresters in Subsector X.2.	
	16/2/17	9.0 pm	The enemy commenced a heavy bombardment of the centre and right of Subsector X.2. using heavy - medium and light trench mortars and some howitzers. The bombardment lasted about 20 minutes and little damage was done. Some lacrymatory gas shells were sent over in their bombardment.	BB.Villers Apt-2ay
"	17/2/17	1.30 am	The enemy opened a second heavy bombardment of the centre and right of Subsector X.2. The bombardment lasted about 15 minutes and a large number of poison shells were sent over from trench mortars. O ration party was caught by the gas in ROBERTS AVENUE and 3 men both gassed before their respirators could be adjusted. These 3 died later and another 8 of the same party were admitted to Hospital	P.C.Villers Apt-2ay

Army Form C. 2118.

WAR DIARY
or
INTELLIGENCE SUMMARY. (9) 2/1 Batt London Rgt.
(Erase heading not required.)

Instructions regarding War Diaries and Intelligence Summaries are contained in F. S. Regs., Part II. and the Staff Manual respectively. Title pages will be prepared in manuscript.

Place	Date	Hour	Summary of Events and Information	Remarks and references to Appendices
FONQUEVILLERS	17/2/17	3.15 am	The enemy opened up a third bombardment of the centre and 1/3 Lt of subsector X2. The bombardment was intense and lasted 15–20 minutes. Very little material damage was done and no casualties were suffered.	R.B.Littler Capt. Adj
"	17/2/17	6 pm	'A' + 'B' Coys commence to evacuate subsectors X2 and march to SUMMER CAMP SOUASTRE for n/pr 17/18=. 'D' Coy evacuates subsectors Y1, Y2 and proceeds to billets at ST AMAND for n/pr 17/18=.	R.B.Littler Capt Adj
SOUASTRE	18/2/17	9.30 am	HQ, 'A' Coy, 'B' Coy leave SOUASTRE } The two parties unite at HENU 'C' Coy, 'D' Coy leave ST AMAND } and the Battalion proceeds by route march to Billets at HALLOY.	R.B.Littler Capt Adj
HALLOY	19/2/17	1.15 pm	The Battalion arrives at HALLOY and occupies "C" Camp. Marching in state 32 Officers 825 Other Ranks	R.B.Littler Capt Adj

T2134. Wt. W708—776. 500000. 4/15. Sir J. C. & S.

WAR DIARY
or
INTELLIGENCE SUMMARY. (10) 2/11 Batt. London Rgt

Army Form C. 2118.

Place	Date	Hour	Summary of Events and Information	Remarks and references to Appendices
HARLOY	23/7/17	12.35 a.m	Following message received from H.Q 175th Bde. (time of despatch 11.50 pm 24/7/17) "Following message received from 58th Division AAA Begins Ludlowian point to the enemy having retired along the front of 5th Corps in rest of 175 Bde AAA All troops will be ready to move at short notice after 5 am tomorrow AAA Message ends AAA All parade for tomorrow including working parties AAA Message ends AAA Battalions will be prepared to march at short notice after 5 am, taking only first line transport AAA Blankets Officers kits and Regimental Stores etc will be left etc etc.	B.Behillers Capt-Adj
"	23/7/17	6.40 am	Informed Bde. that Batt. had been standing-by since 6 am, ready to move.	B.Behillers Capt-Adj
"	23/7/17	9.35 am	Message received from 175. Bde that normal conditions will be resumed.	B.Behillers Capt-Adj

Arth Frank. Lt Col.
Commanding 2/11th Co of London Regt (Finsbury Rifles)

17/58 Vol 3

SECRET

War Diary – 2/1st Batt. Lond Regt.

From: February 27th 1917.
To: March 26th 1917. (Pages 11 – 21 incl.)

Army Form C. 2118.

WAR DIARY
or
INTELLIGENCE SUMMARY.
(Erase heading not required.)

(1) 1/4 Batt'n ?

Instructions regarding War Diaries and Intelligence Summaries are contained in F.S. Regs., Part II. and the Staff Manual respectively. Title pages will be prepared in manuscript.

Place	Date	Hour	Summary of Events and Information	Remarks and references to Appendices
HALLOY	27/2/17	10 a.m.	The Battalion marched out of HALLOY Strength 27 Officers 772 O.R.	BBrullers Tovanby BRwillers Tovanby
GAUDIEMPRE	27/2/17	12.30 pm	The Battalion marched into GAUDIEMPRE and went into billets Strength 27 Officers 777 O.R.	Hellvillers Tovanby
GAUDIEMPRE	28/2/17	6.30 a.m.	The Battalion marched out of GAUDIEMPRE Strength 27 Officers 777 O.R.	
RIVIERE	28/2/17	11. a.m.	HQ 'A' 'C' 'D' Coys marched into RIVIERE and went into Billets Strength 27 Off 780 O.R.	
"	"	12 noon	B Coy proceeded to Ruyse behind Section F and relieved 7/9th Bn London Regt.	BBrullers Copthey
			The Transport proceeded to Transport Lines at BAILLEUVAL.	
			The Commanding Officer, Adj- and Company Commanders proceeded to Section F2 to reconnoitre trenches to be taken over from 1/17th R. West Riding Regiment on 1.3.17.	

Army Form C. 2118.

WAR DIARY
or
INTELLIGENCE SUMMARY.
(Erase heading not required.)

(12) 2/1st London Rgt.

Instructions regarding War Diaries and Intelligence Summaries are contained in F. S. Regs., Part II. and the Staff Manual respectively. Title pages will be prepared in manuscript.

Place	Date	Hour	Summary of Events and Information	Remarks and references to Appendices
SUB-SECTOR F.2	1/3/17	12. noon	"B" Coy relieved in Kaspa by a Company of 2/10th Batt. London Rgt.	BBillon Copies
		2.27 pm	Relief of 11th R. West Riding Regiment in Sector F.2 completed. Dispositions A.D.C. Coys from left to right each with 2 Platoons in firing line and two Platoons in support. "B" Coy in four Platoons Sectors in Reserve line.	BBillon Copies
SUB-SECTOR F.2.	2/3/17 to 4/3/17		Dispositions as above, and no events of importance to record.	BBillon Copies
SUB-SECTOR F.2	5/3/17	2.27 pm	Relieved in Sector F.2. by 2/12th Batt. London Rgt.	BBillon Copies
BELLACOURT	5/3/17	4.0 pm	Arrived at BELLACOURT and went into billets; Bn HQ at the CHATEAU.	BBillon Copies
BELLACOURT	6/3/17	—	Commanding Officer and Company Commanders reconnoitred Subsector D1.	BBillon Copies
SUBSECTOR D1	1/3/17	half pm	2/1st Batt. London Rgt. relieved 2/2nd Batt. London Rgt. in Sub-sector D1.	BBillon Copies

Army Form C. 2118.

WAR DIARY
or
INTELLIGENCE SUMMARY.
(Erase heading not required.)

(13) 7/11 Batt. London Regt

Place	Date	Hour	Summary of Events and Information	Remarks and references to Appendices
Sub Sector D.1.	7/3/17	11:45am	Strength of Battalion on taking over Sub-Sector D.1. 27 Officers 780 O.R. (HQ Personnel 97*: QM Personnel 88*: Non-combatant duties with Coys 37*: Available Rifles 558. *Available in case of emergency. 134. The frontage covered by Sub-sector D.1. is (FREMICOURT Sheet 51c 1.E + 51b S.W.) X 16.05.55 - R33.C.95.40 i.e. 1995 yards. i.e. 2350 yards of fire trench. The Sector is held by Two Companies in the Firing and Support Lines and Two Companies in Reserve each with one Platoon on duty. "A" on Rt. "C" on left. Each of these Companies Res. 2 Platoons in Outpost Groups in Firing line. 2 Platoons in Platoon Posts in Support Line. {"D" on Rt. "B" on left} Relief. The Companies in Firing and Support Lines are relieved by Reserve Companies every 4 days. The Platoons in Outpost positions in Firing Line are relieved by Platoons in Support Posts. every 24 or 48 hours at Company Commander's discretion. Battalion Headquarters moves to Willets at GROSVILLE	See Appendix "A" and plan attached B.Walker Captain
	11/3/17	2.0 pm	The Left Reserve Company (B) moves permanently in CHURCH ST.	

Army Form C. 2118.

WAR DIARY
or
INTELLIGENCE SUMMARY.
(Erase heading not required.)

(IA) 2/1 7/1st Bn. Royal Regt.

Instructions regarding War Diaries and Intelligence Summaries are contained in F.S. Regs., Part II. and the Staff Manual respectively. Title pages will be prepared in manuscript.

Place	Date	Hour	Summary of Events and Information	Remarks and references to Appendices
SUBSECTOR D1.	7/3/17	11.45pm	All quiet since taking over.	B.R.Wilson Capt & Adj
"	8/3/17	8 p.m.	Shells shelling by enemy 4.2".	B.R.Wilson Capt & Adj
"	9/3/17	8 p.m.	Trenches shelled by enemy 4.2" intermittently throughout the day. BELLACOURT and GROSVILLE shelled between 11.30 am & 12.30 pm. Our guns retaliated and silenced him 12.45 pm.	B.R.Wilson Capt & Adj
"	10/3/17	8 p.m.	Our support line from R32c5769 to R32c7545 was heavily shelled between 4.15pm & 4.45pm, nearly 200 shells were have fallen about 50% HE 50% gas. No serious damage done no casualties sustained. Enemy probably trying to locate T.M. which had been cutting his wire during the afternoon. The trenches, which up to now have stood well owing to frost, are rapidly deteriorating now that a thaw has set in.	B.R.Wilson Capt & Adj
"	11/3/17	8 p.m.	Enemy's Artillery has been active during the night 10pm/11th gas shells being constantly thrown into the back portion of the sub-sector. Th wire cutting which has been going	B.R.Wilson Capt & Adj

Army Form C. 2118.

WAR DIARY
or
INTELLIGENCE SUMMARY.
(Erase heading not required.)

(15) 2/t 15 Bn London Rgt

Instructions regarding War Diaries and Intelligence Summaries are contained in F. S. Regs., Part II. and the Staff Manual respectively. Title pages will be prepared in manuscript.

Place	Date	Hour	Summary of Events and Information	Remarks and references to Appendices
SUB SECTOR D1.	11/3/17	9 p.m.	by our T.M. & 18 pdrs. during the 10th has evidently made him apprehensive. Between 10.30 a.m. and 1 p.m. to-day 400 S.O.S. H.2 H.E.shells were fired in the direction of the BELLACOURT – GROSVILLE Road apparently searching for one of our batteries which moved from its position close to the road two days ago.	BB.Artillery Capt + Adj
Trenches			Rain. Rain done serious damage to our trenches DYKE ST. and the trenches round OSIER POST threaten to become impassable.	BB Artillery Capt + Adj
			Patrols. Listening patrols go out with along run 11 p.m. 1 a.m. + 3 a.m. from the support line posts in turn, but have had nothing to report.	BB Artillery Capt + Adj
			"B" "D" Coys have relieved "C" "A" Coys in firing and support lines.	BB Artillery Capt + Adj
SUBSECTOR D1	12/3/17	8 a.m.	A snowstorm in the morning who GROSVILLE and BELLACOURT. O.C. B Coy reports that DYKE ST is impassable for carrying parties. Rations for OSIER POST Platoons must be carried up over the top after dark. The following officers from 9 (Res) Battn. London Rgt. reported for duty.	BB Artillery Capt + Adj
			Lt. R.W. FORD 2/Lt. H.W. MURCH 2/Lt. A.C. SOUTTEN 2/Lt. E.E. SMART.	

T.2134. Wt. W708—776. 500000. 4/15. Sir J. C. & S.

Army Form C. 2118.

WAR DIARY
or
INTELLIGENCE SUMMARY.
(Erase heading not required.)

(16) 2/1st Batt. London Rgt.

Instructions regarding War Diaries and Intelligence Summaries are contained in F. S. Regs., Part II. and the Staff Manual respectively. Title pages will be prepared in manuscript.

Place	Date	Hour	Summary of Events and Information	Remarks and references to Appendices
SUBSECTOR D.1.	13/3/17	8 p.m.	Very little activity during the earlier part of the day. At 7.15 p.m. a small barrage and raid practice was carried out with the object of locating the enemy's machine guns and general behaviour in the event of a raid. The enemy front line trench was barraged for about 100 yards on either side of the point where his wire had been cut at X.2.b.75.40. The barrage consisted of 3 minutes - lifting to support line for 3 minutes and back to front line for 1 minute. 2/Lt G Robins with Sgt Atkins ("C"Co.) and Rfn Blake ("B"Co.) followed up the barrage and ascertained that they could easily have entered the enemy trench only four or five rifles were heard to be firing and four machine guns from points on the flanks. The enemy's response to the barrage was fairly prompt, but consisted of a very desultory shelling of No man's Land and a very large number of rifle shells directed against our batteries. The raiding party returned safely from our trenches.	

Army Form C. 2118.

WAR DIARY
or
INTELLIGENCE SUMMARY.
(Erase heading not required.)

(17) 2/1th Batt. Coro Rgt

Instructions regarding War Diaries and Intelligence Summaries are contained in F.S. Regs., Part II. and the Staff Manual respectively. Title pages will be prepared in manuscript.

Place	Date	Hour	Summary of Events and Information	Remarks and references to Appendices
SUBSECTOR D.	13/3/17	9.a.m.	The G.O.C. Bde inspected the trenches around OSIER POST and decided that the Platoon in occupation should be withdrawn to the support line leaving only a small guard for stores and a weak guard for the T.M. in the OSIER POST position. Other trenches - notably BURNT FARM STREET show signs of deteriorating very rapidly than the small garrison of the trenches can hope to cope with them.	Artillery Cooperay
"	14/3/17	11.25 p.m. 18 mp.	Considerable enemy shelling all day 4.2's 2 minute gun fire. "C" Coy relieving "B" Coy in OSIER POST section taking up new dispositions "A" Coy " "D" Coy in STARFISH POST section	Artillery Cooperay
"	16/3/17	12.29 p.m.	Enemy Artillery has been comparatively silent, our own unusually active, therefore no counts of importance have occurred, weather fine. Aerial activity marked. Hostile aircraft NIL.	Artillery Cooperay

T2134. Wt. W708—776. 500000. 4/15. Sir J. C. & S.

WAR DIARY
or
INTELLIGENCE SUMMARY.
(Erase heading not required.)

Army Form C. 2118.

(18) 2/Lt Ralph Rudorf Lt

Place	Date	Hour	Summary of Events and Information	Remarks and references to Appendices
SUBSECTOR D.1.	16/3/17	11 p.m.	Heavy continuous fire and the trenches are being up slightly. Hostile artillery has been more than usually active, and MG snipers busy. A trench mortar has been brought into action opposite our right sector. Many explosions have been heard during the day in enemy trenches, suggesting the destruction of dug-outs prior to the evacuation of this portion of his line ie between BLAIRVILLE and RANSART.	R.B.Miller Captured
	18/3/17	6 A.m.	During the day the enemy has considerably shelled the neighbourhood of Battn H.Q. and the village of GROSVILLE. Lt Col M.H. GRANT wounded in the foot by a shell splinter at about 7 p.m. at HQ of BURNT FARM STREET. MAJOR W.F.J. SYMONDS assumed command of the Battalion. At 7.0 pm Capt H.G. ASHTON Commanding "A" Coy reported numerous fires in enemy lines, also that no Very lights were being sent up from enemy trenches and that our Lewis Gun and machine gun fire brought no response. At 9.0 p.m. Bde HQ advised strong patrols to reconnoitre German front and second line trenches. Lt P.S. Herbert MC OR and 2/Lt W.G. Atkins -10 DR formed patrols	8.Butler Captured

Army Form C. 2118.

WAR DIARY
or
INTELLIGENCE SUMMARY.
(Erase heading not required.)

(19) 7th Batt. London Regt

Place	Date	Hour	Summary of Events and Information	Remarks and references to Appendices
SIMENCOURT	18/3/17	12.45 am	At 10pm "B" Coy in left sector was ordered to parade in readiness to occupy German trenches between X 2 d 50.90 and X 3 a 00.00 (Fickenpoy) in the event of their being unoccupied by enemy.	
		2.0 am	Patrols report enemy trenches unoccupied. "B" Coy moved forward	
		2.27 am	See Operation Order. NW receiving OC's A, C & D Coys	Shelters Artillery
		5.20 am	"A" and "C" Coys ordered to move forward in right and left of "B" Coy respectively. All three Companies to occupy enemy support line and consolidate. Patrols to be pushed out to locate enemy rear guard.	
		6.30 am	Battalion HQ and "D" Coy moved forward to HEDGE POST in support line. Col GRANT moved forward with Batt. HQ and remained at duty in command of the Battalion.	
		noon.	Work of consolidation proceeding. Patrols have failed to maintain touch with enemy.	
		4 pm	O Special patrol under QT J Young reports line between ADINFER and HENDECOURT	

WAR DIARY or INTELLIGENCE SUMMARY

Army Form C. 2118.

(20) 7th London Regt.

Place	Date	Hour	Summary of Events and Information	Remarks and references to Appendices
SUBSECTOR A.1	18/3/17	4 p.m.	Clear of enemy. The Battalion is ordered to go back to Billets at BELLACOURT, the 173rd Bde having taken over the frontage opposite sub-section D.1.	
BELLACOURT	"	5 p.m.	The Battalion moves to BELLACOURT and is placed under the orders of the C.R.E. for road repair work. Battn. H.Q. at the Chateau BELLACOURT.	
BELLACOURT	19/3/17	9 a.m.	Orders received from C.R.E. to move to Billets at WAILLY.	
		11 a.m.	The following Officers reported for duty from 3/7th Bn London Regt:- 2/Lt. S.J.R.B.SIMMONS (B) 2/Lt. P.G. MITCHELL (D) 2/Lt. S.C. CLAYTON. (A) 2/Lt. R.R. KEELY (A)	2/Lt Wilcox Capt. Adj.
		11 p.m.	The Battalion moved into Billets 'A' 'C' Coys at WAILLY. 'B' 'D' Coys at GROSVILLE. Battn HQ at The Chateau GROSVILLE.	
GROSVILLE	20/3/17	10 a.m.	Day spent in Road Repair work.	
"	21/3/17	"	Day spent in Salvage Stores – ammunition etc from trenches in subsector D.1. Capt. P.R. MANN detailed for duty as Brigade Salvage Officer	
"	22/3/17	9.45 a.m.	The Battalion left GROSVILLE en route for LAHERLIERE.	
LAHERLIERE	"	1 p.m.	The Battalion arrived at LAHERLIERE and went into Billets. HQ at The School.	

T2134. Wt. W708–776. 500000. 4/15. Sir J.C. & S.

WAR DIARY
or
INTELLIGENCE SUMMARY.
(Erase heading not required.)

Army Form C. 2118.

(21) 2/11th Bn London Regt

Place	Date	Hour	Summary of Events and Information	Remarks and references to Appendices
LAHERLIERE	23/3/17	10 a.m.	Cleaning equipment etc.	
	24/3/17	noon	Working parties for R.E. - Inspection of "D" Coy by Commanding Officer.	
			Platoon Training.	
		3 p.m.	The following Officers reported for duties:-	BBhullers Asst Adj
			From 2/17th Bn Lond Regt: 2/Lt E.A.BOYER. 2/Lt V.S.CROSIER. 2/Lt H.J.KEEN.	
			From 9th R.C. Bn Lond Regt: 2/Lt H.N.D.WESSELS. 2/Lt C.F.K.SMITH.	
LAHERLIERE	25/3/17	9.30 a.m.	The Battalion marched out of LAHERLIERE en route for HALLOY.	
HALLOY.		1.15 p.m.	Arrived at HALLOY and occupied "C" Camp.	BBhullers Asst Adj
			Lt. Col. M.H.GRANT admitted to No.43 C.C.S. Major W.F.J.SYMONDS assumes command.	
HALLOY.	26/3/17		Day spent in cleaning up, bathing and Platoon training.	

W.F.J. Symonds
Major Regt
OC 2/11 London Regt

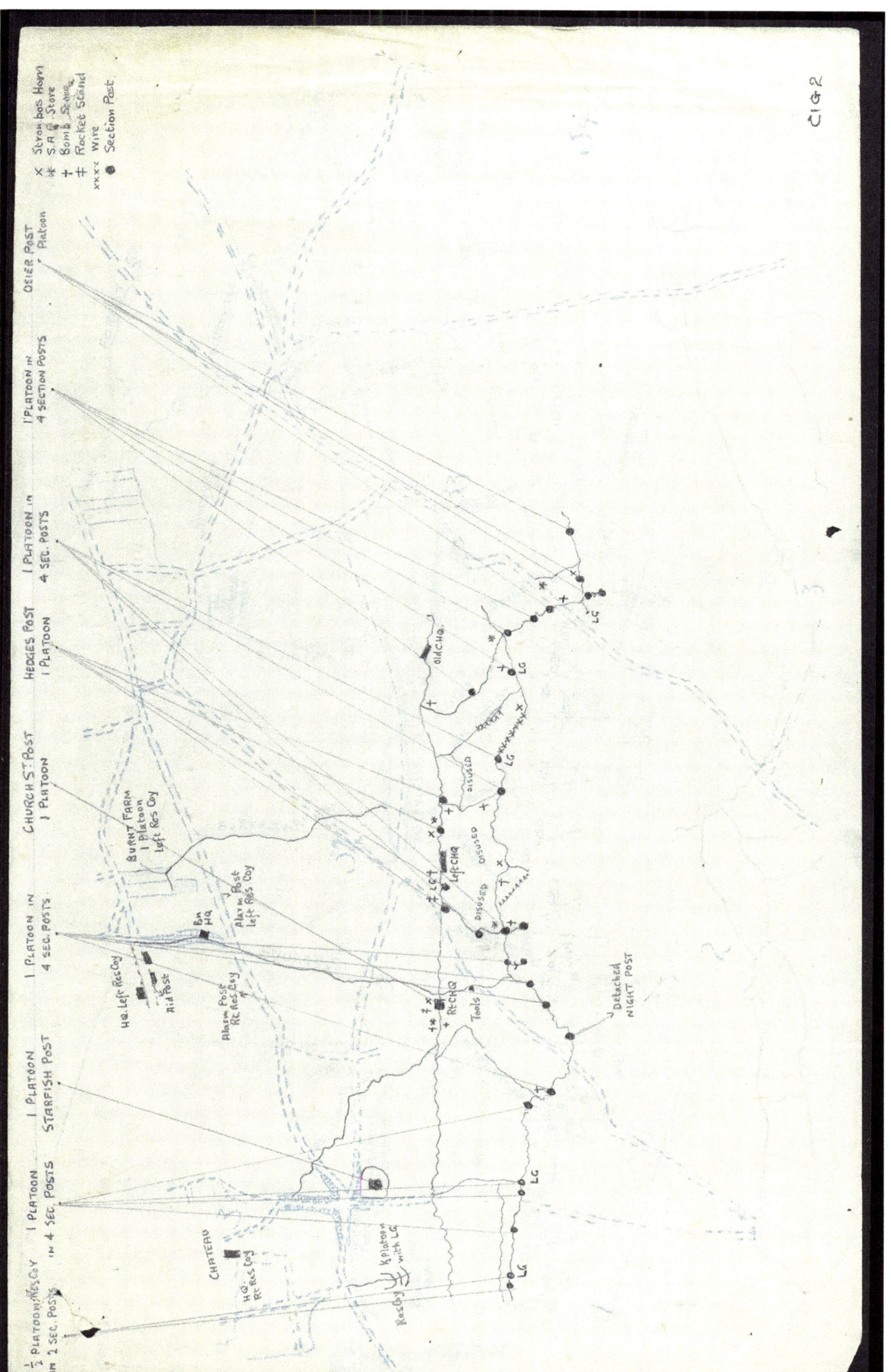

175/58 Vol 4

SECRET

WAR DIARY.

2/11th Battn. London Regiment.

From :- March 27th 1917.
To :- April 26th 1917.

75 Adv

Army Form C. 2118.

WAR DIARY
or
INTELLIGENCE SUMMARY.
(Erase heading not required.)

(22) 7/11 - Batt. Rone. Regt.

Instructions regarding War Diaries and Intelligence Summaries are contained in F.S. Regs., Part II. and the Staff Manual respectively. Title pages will be prepared in manuscript.

Place	Date	Hour	Summary of Events and Information	Remarks and references to Appendices
HALLOY	27/3/17	5pm	Platoon training. Bathing during the day	
	28/3/17	9am	Inspection of Anti-gas appliances by Divisional Gas Officer ?	
			Platoon training as per Programme B.S.143	
	29/3/17	6pm	Platoon training during the day. Coy's Willcase departed for duty	
			as Commandants of Divisional Depot Batts. Bourguedouson, R & ?	
			Noble took over duties of Adjutants of Batts.	
	30/3/17	9am	Platoon training during the day	
	31/3/17	5pm	Batts. scheme in Range valley. Brief 2/Lt Jenis departed for	
			duty with 2PM. 2/Lt Spencer returned to duty with Batts.	
KARLY	1/4/17	10.40am	the Batts. moved to KARLY via the following ? route E of Esperance	
			Doullens Station Georges Chateau BARLY. Batts. billeted	
	2/4/17	5pm	Batts. moved out of Barley @ 10.15 on route for BURRE AU BOIS	
			via the following Remaistre PROHEN WEVEN'S MOEUX BARLY	
			billeted in BURE AU BOIS	
BURE AU BOIS	3/4/17	4.30pm	Day spent in interior economy & 2 hrs drill	
	4/4/17	5pm	Day spent in platoon training	

WAR DIARY
or
INTELLIGENCE SUMMARY.

(Erase heading not required.)

Army Form C. 2118.

(23) 2/11 Battn London Regt

Place	Date	Hour	Summary of Events and Information	Remarks and references to Appendices
BOIRE AU BOIS	5/4/17	8 AM	Battalion marched out of Boire au Bois to Cross Roads, south of MAMOR FARM, where Battalion embussed for Bus les Artois, arriving at 5 pm & occupied JUNIPER CAMP. 58th Division transferred to 5th Army.	
BUS LES ARTOIS	6/4/17	5 pm	Platoon training during the day. C.O. inspected anti gas appliances of Battn.	
"	7/4/17	8 am	Battn as a working party, as fatigue parties under R.E., cleaning railway lines &c.	
"	8/4/17	8.45 AM	Battn marched out of Bus les Artois to MIRAUMONT by the following route: Fatigue parties authorised Beaumont Hamel, Beaucourt Station, MIRAUMONT. Arrived for the night.	
MIRAUMONT	9/4/17	7.30 7 am	Battn moved out of MIRAUMONT for working party at ACHIET LE PETIT (Sheet 57c G 20.c 58) under Canadian overseas Railway Corps for railway work. On conclusion of work Battn encamped at ACHIET LE PETIT under canvas.	
ACHIET LE PETIT	10/4/17	5 pm	Whole Battn working parties. No 1 (3 companys) at ACHIET Station - South end. No 2 (1 company) railway work at LE GRAND Station - North end.	

Army Form C. 2118.

WAR DIARY
or
INTELLIGENCE SUMMARY.
(Erase heading not required.)

(24) 2/11 London Regt

Place	Date	Hour	Summary of Events and Information	Remarks and references to Appendices
ACHIET LE PETIT	10/4/17	5pm	ACHIET LE GRAND under O/C with Bath CRT (No 3) Working Party 3 pours, 9 20 men under Town Major Achiet le Petit. (No 4) Working Party of 15 OR under OC Supply column @ RSO ACHIET-LE GRAND	
"	11/4/17	5pm	Three companies on Working Parties. A 115 for work at ACHIET LE GRAND Railway station, A Coy with Canadian Railway Transport at ACHIET LE GRAND, also 15 OR under OC supply return @ RSO. ACHIET LE GRAND & 23 OR with Town Major, ACHIET LE PETIT 40 "C Company" Platoon training	
"	12/4/17	5pm	Whole Batn Platoon training	
"	13/4/17	5pm	A & D Companies' working parties A & D 180 OR under Canadian Overseas Railway Corps, B Coy 100 OR at ACHIET LE GRAND ST" under Canadian R/Y Transport. Bn of Coy's Platoon training	
"	14/4/17	6pm	Platoon training A Coy 100 OR working Party 5 as ashen a former Railway Station from 130 pm. D Coy turned out of Camp @ 1pm as Escort as carrying Party for front line, reporting for Guide at MORY at Batn Church parade 9 AM of day cleaning up. Working Party of	
	15/4/17	6pm		

Army Form C. 2118.

WAR DIARY
or
INTELLIGENCE SUMMARY.
(Erase heading not required.)

(25) 2/11 London Regt.

Place	Date	Hour	Summary of Events and Information	Remarks and references to Appendices
ACHIET LE PETIT	15/4/17	6 pm	3 journeys 150 O.R for Tour trays ACHIET LE PETIT	
	16/4/17	5 am	Batln on working parties No 1 (100 OR) B Coy under 4th Bn C.O.R.E. at Achiet le Grand Railway Sidn No 2 200 OR A.H.C Coys under to O.R. 9th Railway work near PUISIEUX No 3 13 Coy 200 OR railway work at A.30.D.10 (Sheet 57C)	
	17/4/17	6 am	Coy training in the attack	
	18/4/17	5 am	Batln on working parties railway work under LO.R. 66 & C.R.T	
	19/4/17	6 am	Platoon training during the morning Bath practice attack on German system of trenches south of Logeast Wood in the afternoon Platoon training. A Coy (130 OR) working party under R.E. (Construction Co) ACHIET LE PETIT. C Coy (130 OR) working party crossing BAPAUME - under 4th Bn Canadian Engrs. on light Railway. ERVILLERS Rd	
	20/4/17	6 am	Two companies working parties A Coy (130 OR) for work under C.R.T at MORY from 11am to 4pm. B Coy (130 OR) for work under C.R.T at Logeast B.26 & 1080 (57C Sheet) from 11am	

Army Form C. 2118.

WAR DIARY
or
INTELLIGENCE SUMMARY. (26) 2/11 London Regt
(Erase heading not required.)

Instructions regarding War Diaries and Intelligence Summaries are contained in F. S. Regs., Part II. and the Staff Manual respectively. Title pages will be prepared in manuscript.

Place	Date	Hour	Summary of Events and Information	Remarks and references to Appendices
ACHIET LE PETIT	21/4/17	6pm	Review of Batn. Platoon training.	
"	22/4/17	"	Whole Batn. Church Parade. Inspection by Commanding Officer.	
	22/4/17		Rest of day. Short'n cleaning up & bathing. Three Companies Working parties.	
			B) day 150 OR & B (300 OR) under RTO ACHIET LE GRAND from MIDNIGHT to 8 AM. A.C. that B (300 OR) under RTO ACHIET LE GRAND from 8 AM to them. B" of B" Coy Baileu Training Trench Mortar ammunition (15 OR in parties) at present 14 L. for diggers. Two Working parties formed 1st (150 OR) B Coy for work under	
	24/4/17		Road Commandant D Coy. Plat ACHIET LE GRAND No 2 (150 OR) A Coy? Labour Cp. for work under RTO ACHIET LE GRAND from them to midnight.	
"	25/4/17	8pm	Platoon training as per Brigade B.M.K 363. Platoons inspected at work by M.General Inskrive & Bdier Shoot. O Coy Inspection of Physical Training & Bayonet fighting.	
	26/4/17	5pm	Whole Batn. Platoon training. Work of Ampts & Plat Persquing Platoon by Lieut 5th Army Corps. Batn. inspected while training by Gen. of 5th Army Corps Staff.	

Army Form C. 2118.

WAR DIARY
or
INTELLIGENCE SUMMARY.
(Erase heading not required.)

(27) 2/1 London Regt.

Place	Date	Hour	Summary of Events and Information	Remarks and references to Appendices
Actict to Part I	28/4/17	5pm	Sqdn Commander at 11.30 P.M. Afternoon Bolton Outpost scheme	Whole The field

SCHEME FOR THE DEFENCE OF SUBSECTOR D1
BY
LT. COL. M. H. GRANT
COMMANDING 2/11TH BATTALION LONDON REGIMENT.

(i) The Subsector is occupied by four Companies:-
   Two in the firing and support lines,
   Two in Reserve.

(ii) (a) <u>Line of Observation</u>. The Companies in the firing and support lines each maintain eight section posts in the firing line, i.e. two complete Platoons, and two Platoons in strong posts in the Support Line.

   (b) <u>Support Line</u>. The Company on the left garrisons:-
       OSIER POST and HEDGES POST.
   The Company on the right garrisons:-
       CHURCH STREET Post and STARFISH POST
   and in addition to maintaining the eight section posts in the firing line, will find a party of three bombers for duty at No. 11 M.G. Post.

   (c) <u>Reserve Line</u>. The Companies in Reserve will be billeted at BELLACOURT and GROSVILLE.
       The Company in Reserve at BELLACOURT maintains a post of one N.C.O. and three men with Lewis Gun and a section of Riflemen in the firing line at a point on the extreme right of the Subsector, about 400 yards N. of the BELLACOURT – RANSART Road.
       This post is responsible for maintaining communication with the Battalion on its right.
       This Company will also keep a Lewis Gun Team at BOUNDARY POST and in the event of an Alarm, will man both BOUNDARY POST and the BELLACOURT WOOD work with one Platoon each.

       The Company in Reserve at GROSVILLE will keep a permanent garrison of one Platoon in BURNT FARM POST.

(iii) <u>Patrols.</u> All patrols forward will be found from the troops in the Support Line strong posts.
       Lateral Communication between section posts and Support line strong posts will be maintained by patrols under arrangements to be made by O's C. Coys. in the firing and support lines. O.C. left Company will be responsible for maintaining communication with the Battalion on the left and O.C., Reserve Coy. in BELLACOURT will be responsible for maintaining lateral communication with the Battalion on the right.

(iv) <u>Alarm Posts for Reserves.</u> In the event of Alarm or Attack, the Reserve Companies and H.Q. Personnel will move to their Alarm Posts as follows:-
   (a) The Company from BELLACOURT (less Lewis Gun Team (1 N.C.O. and three men) and rifle section in firing line, one Platoon in BOUNDARY POST and one Platoon in the BELLACOURT WOOD work) will move via SHRAPNEL CORNER to the junction at the SHRAPNEL CORNER – BRETTENCOURT Road with CHURCH STREET and will form up facing N.E. with its left on the road junction – extended to two paces with twenty paces between Platoons and will await orders.

Page 2.

(iv) **Alarm Posts for Reserves (Continued).**

    (b) The Company in GROSVILLE less one Platoon in BURNT FARM POST and will proceed via CHURCH STREET and form up on the SHRAPNEL CORNER - BRETTENCOURT ROAD with its right on the junction of that road with CHURCH STREET - facing S.E. - extended to two paces, with twenty paces between platoons, and will await orders.

    (c) The H.Q. Personnel will form up in CHURCH STREET in file facing S.E. outside the Battalion Orderly Room. They will then be disposed according to requirements.

(v) IN THE EVENT OF ATTACK the section posts in the firing line will stand fast. In no ordinary case will the garrison of the front line fall back on the support line posts. Should, however, they be forced back, they will on retirement fill in all approaches to the strong posts with entanglements thrown into the communication trenches. For this purpose knife-rests etc. must be kept handy inside all parapets.

    The garrisons of strong posts will under no circumstances be used for counter attack.

    If the front line should be occupied by the enemy, he will be dealt with by the Reserve Companies under the direct orders of the O.C. Battalion.

    The garrisons of the strong posts in the Reserve Line i.e. BURNT FARM - BELLACOURT WOOD and BOUNDARY POSTS will stand fast in their posts with the object of holding up the attack until the arrival of the two Battalions in Brigade Reserve, three hours after the receipt of warning.

GENERAL. The scheme is purely that of an Outpost Battalion, with the normal functions of reconnaissance, deception and delay. Instructions for the two first-named roles are embodied in attached.

                                                  Lt. Col.,
                    Commdg., 2/XIth Battn. London Regt.
                            (Finsbury Rifles).

Army Form C. 2118.

17/5-8   Vol 5

WAR DIARY
or
INTELLIGENCE SUMMARY.
(Erase heading not required.)

SECRET

WAR DIARY.

2/XIIth Batt'n London Regt.

Volume IV

From: April 27th 1917
To: May 26 - 1917

Army Form C. 2118.

WAR DIARY
or
INTELLIGENCE SUMMARY.   (28) 2/11 London Regt

(Erase heading not required.)

Place	Date	Hour	Summary of Events and Information	Remarks and references to Appendices
ACHIET LE PETIT	27/4/17	5 am	Batn inspection full marching order, transport in rear. Bgd Brigadier Gen follows. BSO. Afternoon Brigade surprise attack on German disused trenches and [?] of Logeast Wood	Appx. the Bgde
"	28/4/17		3 coys working parties No 1 Working party 300 OR (A & D) for work under R.T.O. Achiet Le Grand reporting @ 8 a.m. No 2 Working Party (150 OR C Coy) for work under R.T.O. Achiet Le Grand. B Coy. Bathing Station cleaning bathing during the day	Appx. the Bgde
"	29/4/17	"	Batn Church Parade. Rest of day spent cleaning up Camp & equipment. Brigadier inspected Camp	Appx. the Bgde
"	30/4/17	"	Batn employed on Working parties 'B' Coy under R.T.O. Achiet Le Grand. A Coy under Town Major Miraumont 2 platoons C Coy under HQ B.C.R.T. 2 under A.D.L.R.S. at Achiet Le Grand. D Coy under Town Major Achiet Le Petit.	Appx. the Bgde
"	1/5/17	"	Bn employed on working parties. C Coy under Town Major. Miraumont D Coy under R.T.O. Achiet Le Grand 1 platoon A. under T.M. Achiet Le Petit	Appx. the Bgde

WAR DIARY
INTELLIGENCE SUMMARY (29) 2/11 London Regt

Army Form C. 2118.

Place	Date	Hour	Summary of Events and Information	Remarks and references to Appendices
ACHIET LE PETIT	2/5/17	4pm	Battn on working parties. No 1. 300 OR under RTO ACHIET LE GRAND @ 8am ¬ 150 OR @ 4pm	
	3/5/17		Morning platoon training officers Battn en attack GOC inspected one platoon of 'B' Coy	
	4/5/17		Battn moved from ACHIET LE PETIT to VRAUCOURT at 1.30pm	
		9 at 10pm relieved the 5th Battn Australians in outpost line A Coy sent 2 platoons to forward outposts at points C.18.d.33 ³ C.24.c.88 ² 2 two platoons on support in running trench C.24.c.50. B Coy on road at points C.29.d.88 C.6 to B Coys in sunken road from C.24.d.12 to 30.d.18. (54° NW ———)	
54° NW 20000 C.30 A 28	5/6/17	11pm	All quicks after taking over, and at 10 pm the gcs Bn of the Regt relieved the Battn. Who moved forward & relieved the 56 Bn Australians Inf, relief being completed at 2 am (6/5/17). Dispositions were as follows:- 11 platoons in front line of sunken road from II13.A.0030 to D14.C.3030. 6 platoons on left front sector under Capt Hunt (platoons of 6 7 14 15 platoons of B) &	

WAR DIARY or INTELLIGENCE SUMMARY.

Army Form C. 2118.

(30) 2/1 London Regt

Place	Date	Hour	Summary of Events and Information	Remarks and references to Appendices
57cNW1/40000 C.24.d.Y.6.5.	5/5/17	10 pm	5 Platoons under Capt Smith (4 platoons B & No 16 Platoon) Relief of two companies D 15 C.75. During the night great activity & artillery fire by both sides on our extreme left. Two Germans dropped bombs & mortars on D.13.D.9.4. Above wounding 2/Lt. 4P Ruell & killing 3 ORs	Above [initials] / Appx s
	6/5/17	4 pm	Day comparatively quiet. Little shrapnel from enemy. German trench mortars & artillery shelled front lines to Coys having casualties of 1 OR killed & 2 wounded.	Above [initials] / Appx s
"	7/5/17	"	Day fairly quiet. Very little artillery fire from enemy. Rather quieter active. Ym on right of B Coy very active during the night & enemy artillery active.	Above [initials] / Appx s
"	8/5/17	12 pm	Little artillery on either side. 1 at 10 pm the 2/9.15th started relieving this Bn. who took over Brigade reserve posn in right sector in sunken road C.24.d.12.6. & C.30.d.18. Relief & occupation of reserve line completed at 1.45 AM 9/5/17	Above [initials] / Appx s
C.30.A.28	9/5/17	11 pm	Day comparatively quiet. Enemy's artillery shelled sunken Rd. by Brigade HdQrs at (C.29.A.5.2.) wounding two of B Coys	Above [initials] / Appx s

WAR DIARY
or
INTELLIGENCE SUMMARY.

(31) 2/4 Can Regt

Army Form C. 2118.

Place	Date	Hour	Summary of Events and Information	Remarks and references to Appendices
57C.NW from C20 A28	9/5/17	11/2am	Cooks also 3 OR's of "A" Coy wounded with shrapnel.	
	10/5/17		Day very quiet, very little artillery. B.H.Q. boys carrying wire under R.E's from point D.19 E.22 from 11pm to 3am to [illegible] running in front of support line.	
	11/5/17		Day very quiet. German artillery shelled MORCHIES heavily at 9.30am. Battn relieved by 31st Bn Australian by @ 10pm. Proceeded to point I.y.c.8.6 for the night occupying Bd Res trenches. Bugby— Yars [illegible] line from I.y.a.3 to H.6A.4.5. Relief completed by 1am. ? New trenches occupied by 5pm (12/5/17) Bd Sup after relief continued on work under R.E. wiring in front of Support line.	
T.Y.C.66 FAVREUIL	12/5/17		Battn marched to FAVREUIL. Encamped for the night.	
	13/5/17		Day spent in cleaning up.	
	14/5/17	9am	Company training during the day.	
	15/5/17	3.30pm	Battn marched out of FAVREUIL to Brigade Camp at BIHUCOURT 145th Brigade being in Divisional Reserve to Div front from	

WAR DIARY or INTELLIGENCE SUMMARY

Army Form C. 2118.

(32) 2/4 London Regt

Place	Date	Hour	Summary of Events and Information	Remarks and references to Appendices
Bihucourt	15/5/17	5 pm	U 23. c 80 to the Ecoust – Bullecourt Rd West of Bullecourt. Company training during the day. Orders received	Hostile artillery
"	16/5/17	"	The Bn would relieve the Bn in Right front sub-sector	Hostile active
"	17/5/17	"	Company training during the day, including firing on the range. Orders received on 16th re relief of Right front sub-sector postponed for 48 hrs	Hostile active
"	18/5/17	10 pm	Battn attended Gas demonstration at point Y 22 A. Afternoon Company training.	Hostile artillery and rifle
"	19/5/17	2.30 pm	Battn moved from Bihucourt to Transport lines B 30.A. arrived 4.45 pm. At 8.30 pm the Bn proceeded by platoons to relieve the 2/4th Batn London Regt in Reserve line of Bullecourt Sector U 23 c 80 to U 22 c 92	Hostile active
	20/5/17	11 am	Bn in Reserve lines to front line Relieve the 2/1st & 2/2nd Battalions. Coy rest on frontage U 23 c 80 to U 22 c 92	Hostile active
	21/5/17	3 am	ABCD in line 2 platoons of each Coy in support line, A Coy on right from U23c 80 to U23 c 52, B from U 23 c 52 to U 23 c 34 C from U 23 c 24 to U 22 a 64, D from U 22 a 64 to U 22 a 03. Bn HQ U 29 a 77	

Army Form C. 2118.

WAR DIARY
or
INTELLIGENCE SUMMARY.
(Erase heading not required.)

(33) 2/1 Lon Regt

Instructions regarding War Diaries and Intelligence Summaries are contained in F. S. Regs, Part II. and the Staff Manual respectively. Title pages will be prepared in manuscript.

Place	Date	Hour	Summary of Events and Information	Remarks and references to Appendices
BULLECOURT RIGHT SECTOR	2d/1/		Trenches were in a very bad state owing decomposed bodies lying about. Trenches were precariously shellholes joined together.	Whyte
			Enemy Artillery shelled our front trenches intensively from 3.45 - 4.30 AM with shrapnel & H.E. causing several casualties. Total for 24 hrs 3 killed & 19 wounded ORs	
	2d/2	3.A.M.	Day used in clearing up trenches, sorting equipment, &c. Enemy's Artillery again active shelling the whole trench system from 1.15 AM to 1.05 AM, 3.45 - 4.30 AM. Maintained a desultory shelling of dug-outs during the day. Casualties 2/Lt Herbert killed 2/Lt WAY, MURCH & 2/Lt CEK SMITH wounded. ORs killed 3 & 19 OR's wounded. During bombardments enemy used many signals presumably Red, Green flares, which burst into two clusters of flairs when in the air. PATROLS sent out to Coy frontages, but no information gathered. 2/Lt Herbert was killed by shells on starting off with Patrol to search Boers trench from 22d O3 to 22c U6	

Army Form C. 2118.

WAR DIARY
or
INTELLIGENCE SUMMARY.
(Erase heading not required.)

(34) 2/4 Lon Regt

Place	Date	Hour	Summary of Events and Information	Remarks and references to Appendices
BULLECOURT RIGHT SECTOR	22/5/17	3 AM	Snipers very active ours causing several casualties in CT running from C5.A.52 to U29a 94	Noble 2/Lt + 9pt rough
		12 M/D	Enemy Artillery again very active during shortness 38's on support & front line. Also enemy "Whizz Bangs" & 104mm apparently coming from direction of QUEANT	
			Signals were again used, 7 flares were invariably used before Bombardment commenced.	Hartle 2/Lt + adjt
			Movement Various small parties of Germans were seen during the day at about U16.a.09	
			PATROLS Both of the boys patrolled to our front but nothing of importance to note. Daylight patrol went out under 2/Lt Wy Richards from U22.d.03 onwards U22.B.63. but tried to return	
			owing to snipers	
			British party active during the day. Casualties 6 OR killed 9 ORs wounded	
22/5/17			Enemy Artillery much less active, Snipers became more but out	

Army Form C. 2118.

WAR DIARY
or
INTELLIGENCE SUMMARY.
(Erase heading not required.)

(35) 2/11 Bn Can Regt

Place	Date	Hour	Summary of Events and Information	Remarks and references to Appendices
BULLECOURT RIGHT SECTOR	23/5/17	12 mid	of action. Enemy much quieter. Casualties 1 OR killed 3 wounded	Whittle 2 Lieut Bn Recds
	24/5/17		Sector Quiet. Salvage work being carried on units Bn relieved by 2/10 Bn at 11 pm & proceeded back to support lines, 4 time	
			from burrows C.4 C.5.C.6. B. Bay Central to two from burrows C.4 C.5.C.6. B. Bay Central to two C.5. A+4 C. IBn 4.12. NOREUIL ROAGATE RD. D. C.10 aid Dump the night 2 Lt J A Suckle was wounded & during day tough 3 OR killed & 4 wounded. Enemy's artillery active during night	Whittle 2 Lt
"	25/5/17	11 pm	Quiet day in Support line. A Coy carrying pasty (ration) to 2/12 shelled & 5 slightly posn shelled Casualties 1 OR killed 8 ORs wounded. 2/8 Bn relieved Bn and Bn proceeded to Transport lines @ C30 A central. Journeyed for the night	Whittle 2 Lt Bn Recds
C30 A Central	26/5/17	11 pm	Day spent in resting men & cleaning up. At 7.30 pm Bn moved from Transport lines to MORY SUNK over camp of 2/6 Bn Can Regt	Whittle 2 Lt Bn Recds

T2134. Wt. W708—776. 500000. 4/15. Sir J. C. & S.

Army Form C. 2118.

WAR DIARY
or
INTELLIGENCE SUMMARY.
(Erase heading not required.)

Confidential

War Diary

2/XI Battⁿ London Regt

Volume 5

From :-
May 24th
to :- 30th June

WAR DIARY
INTELLIGENCE SUMMARY

Army Form C. 2118.

(36) 2/11 Durham Regt

Place	Date	Hour	Summary of Events and Information	Remarks and references to Appendices
MORY	24/5/17	10pm	Company "Specialist" training during the day. Church service held during the morning. 2Lt G.G. Smart left Bn for duty with Chinese Labour Bn on 25/5/17	
	28/5/17		Company "Specialist" training during the day.	
	29/5/17		— do — 2 platoons of "C" Coy working party under 2nd Major MOE?	
	30/5/17		Company "Specialist" training during the day	
	31/5/17		Working parties found during the day "B" Coy 60 ORs for work under 503 R.E. Field Coy., "C" Coy 60 ORs under 503 R.E. & Coy "D" Coy 3 NCOs & 50 men under Town Major MORY. A Coy 2. Platoons for drawing range under Lieut Field.	
	1/6/17	6pm	Company Training. "A" & "D" Coys inspected by Commanding Officer in fighting order	
	2/6/17		Company training from barns during the day. Church parade @ 9.30AM. Bath moved from camp at MORY	
	3/6/17		to Transport lines @ C.30.A central @ 2.15pm 9.15pm moved	

Army Form C. 2118.

WAR DIARY
or
INTELLIGENCE SUMMARY. (37) 2/4 Battn London Regt
(Erase heading not required.)

Place	Date	Hour	Summary of Events and Information	Remarks and references to Appendices
MORY	3/4/17	4pm	to relieve 2/5 Bn London Regt in Bullecourt Right front sub sector. Dispositions given with Front line from Right to Left: B Coy A from U23c to U23c 2930, C Coy U23c 2930 to U23d 1030 D Coy from U23d 1030 to U23d 1020. A Coy in support trench from U23c 6060 to U28d 5050. B Coy 2 Platoons in front line two Platoons in support trench slong U20 from 50 X's Relief completed at 2.5 am. Held trench as casualties. Artillery Slight Bombardment of our line about by mm & 4.2 mortars otherwise front line quiet	
BULLECOURT Rt FRONT SUB SECTOR	5/4/17	4AM	Artillery (Hostile) During the day 4.2 & Bullecourt & Ecoust increased. 4.2 & 5.9 also shelled line near U23c 3010 and killed two 4.2's also support line near U23c 3010 and killed some. 2nd Lieut Poiriers with heavy column to be for ration 2/nd Lieut Poirier & Supplies were killed during the night. Officer Patrols sent by 2nd Lieut Haig & 2/Lt Stoney travelled to within 20 yards during the night but no information obtained. Casualties 4 m.r	

Army Form C. 2118.

WAR DIARY
or
INTELLIGENCE SUMMARY. (38) 2/11 London Regt
(Erase heading not required.)

Instructions regarding War Diaries and Intelligence Summaries are contained in F. S. Regs., Part II. and the Staff Manual respectively. Title pages will be prepared in manuscript.

Place	Date	Hour	Summary of Events and Information	Remarks and references to Appendices
BULLECOURT FRONT RIGHT SUB SECTOR	6/9/17	4pm	Quiet day. Very little activity on either side. Hostile snipers machine guns active. Casualties 2 killed 2 wounded ORs.	
	7/9/17		Baths allowed to front line Coy. 2/4 Lee Dow Regt. that over. Other positions.	
	8/9/17		Positions A. Coy Rly Embankment Cub 35.80 – O.L.6.80 B3 Norven – Battle Pit C.9.20.5 – C.15.3.3 D Valley post C.24.2.0 C.14.2.0 HQ @ C.24.2.5 Rly. compted by 2/20th 96/7 Bruss Sly 1/4 Sussex 1 Coy Essex no Div of Inf Works artillery	
BULLECOURT SUPPORT RIGHT SUB SECTOR	9/9/17	10am	Very heavy hostile artillery. Working Parties 303rd Pho Company from 10am to 4pm, Suburban party morning trench B Coy 2 platoons of D worked Pho from 9.15pm to 2.30am Evening carrying working Parties for work in front of BULLECOURT Rly Embankment I Casualty Accidentally wounded by bomb	
	10/9/17		Working parties to try and under Rly Embankment Coy 2nd	

Army Form C. 2118.

WAR DIARY
or
INTELLIGENCE SUMMARY. (39) 2/11 Bn London Regt
(Erase heading not required.)

Place	Date	Hour	Summary of Events and Information	Remarks and references to Appendices
BULLECOURT RIGHT SUPPORT SUB SECTOR	10/6/17	10pm	"B" Coy runners "B" Coy wiring in front of Rly Embankment from 9.45pm to 2.30am 11/6/17. "D" Coy wiring opening out Gordon Switch from 9.30pm to 2.30am 11/6/17. 3 ORs wounded incl "B" Coy on Noreuil Ecoust Rd.	Noted W. G. Mc
	11/6/17		Slight shelling of Ecoust. "C" Coy working party under PC. Wiring Bullecourt Rly Emb. Trench from 10pm to 11pm. 2 Platoons "D" under PC defending Bullecourt Avenue 9.30am to 2.30pm. 2 Platoons of "D" working on Right Coys area from 9.15pm to 2.30am 12/6. "B" Coy 9.45pm to 2.30am wiring Rly wiring in front of Bullecourt Rly Embankment. 2 OR's casualty.	Noted
	12/6/17		Very little enemy activity. 2 Platoons of "D" Coy wiring on embankment. Ammunition from 11pm to 2.30am 13/6/17. "B" Coy & 2 Platoons "D" Coy wiring in front of Bullecourt Rly Emb. from 9.45pm to 2.30am 13/6/17. "B" Coy digging in front under PC from 9.30pm to 2.30am.	Noted W. G. Mc
	13/6/17		Quiet day. "B" Coy from Chateau D. wiring under PC in front of Bullecourt Rly Emb. from 9.45pm to 1.15am. 210 Batn.	3.0 aug

T2134. Wt. W708—776. 500000. 4/15. Sir J. C. & S.

Army Form C. 2118.

WAR DIARY
or
INTELLIGENCE SUMMARY.

(Erase heading not required.)

(40) 2/11 Bn London Regt

Place	Date	Hour	Summary of Events and Information	Remarks and references to Appendices
BIHUCOURT RIGHT SUPPORT SUB SECTOR	13/4/17	10am	Carried out raid on BOIS TRENCH between UC5b & U28c05. Raiding party consisted of 3 offrs & 60 ORs, minus supporting party on Enemy's captured line & 2 ORs. Our casualties 1 Offr wounded & 4 ORs.	note
	14/4/17		Quiet day. Bn relieved in line by 4 Bn. Gen'l Duke.	
	15/4/17	3PM	Bn in billets, proceeded to camp 4 mrs 2 mi. B near Relief received by 2nd Bn Bn Borders the 14th. Casualty received during the 14th.	note
MORY	15/4/17		Also 2 Horses in Evening dull & wet day. Bathing men Orders received from Brigade that Batln would probably come under orders of 20 C 174th Inf Brigade at 3 pm. Orders received to proceed to St LEGER. Took over billets of 2/5 Bn Lon Regt. Arrived ST LEGER 10.45pm. I remained for night. A & C Coys proceeded to U 25 b 33 to report to Col Bartusky. Going down further east of 173rd Inf Brigade. Casualties 3ORs. to this party. No further orders from 174th Brigade. Bn on reaching St Leger found billets of 2/5 taken over by 2/4 before our arrival own	note

T2134. Wt. W708-776. 500000. 4/15. Sir J.C. & S.

Army Form C. 2118.

WAR DIARY
or
INTELLIGENCE SUMMARY. (41) 2/1 Bn London Regt

(Erase heading not required.)

Instructions regarding War Diaries and Intelligence Summaries are contained in F. S. Regs., Part II. and the Staff Manual respectively. Title pages will be prepared in manuscript.

Place	Date	Hour	Summary of Events and Information	Remarks and references to Appendices
ST LEGER	16/6/17	—	MORY - ST LEGER RD - indigons for the night	Stopps to radio
	17/6/17	10 pm	A.C.D Coys W.O.K over trilles hus St Leger during the morning A.C. Coys returned from C.B. arriving @ 8 a.m. 4 pm orders received from 175th Brigade to return to Camp at MORY. Battn reached Camp @ 9.15 pm	Stopps to radio
MORY	18/6/17	8pm	Company Training during the day. Barrage BND Coys (165 O.R's 3 offs) carrying party from 11 pm to 3 am 19/6/17, carrying from BULLECOURT CRATER to CRUCIFIX, moving dumps of stores & wetis & for Brigade attack	Stopps to radio
"	19/6/17	10/2am	During the morning 160 training. Afternoon C.O. W B Coys supplied for 2/10 attack training. Brigade orders for attack on 2/22 fine cancelled	Stopps average
"	20/6/17		Coy Training during the day	More no rain
"	21/6/17	10/2am	Coy training during the morning. Whole Battn working party under 2L't Cong Rbn on C.T. running from Coy HQ's 85 to OCP 75 Ho from 8 am to 2 am 22/6/17. 2/Lt Cong off, 2/Lt Wallers off, 2/Lt Lancer off 2/Lt fittens & another fraom reported for duty.	Stopps to rain

T2134. Wt. W708—776. 500000. 4/15. Sir J.C. & S.

Army Form C. 2118.

WAR DIARY
or
INTELLIGENCE SUMMARY.
(Erase heading not required.)

(42) 2/4 London Regt

Instructions regarding War Diaries and Intelligence Summaries are contained in F.S. Regs., Part II. and the Staff Manual respectively. Title pages will be prepared in manuscript.

Place	Date	Hour	Summary of Events and Information	Remarks and references to Appendices
MORY	22/6/17	7pm	Men rested during the day. Musketry exercises conducted in the evening.	
	23/6/17	10am	Company firing during the day.	
	24/6/17		B.C.D. Coys firing on range.	
			Church service during the morning. At 3.15 pm Bath parade.	
			Parade of 20 to Wardrobes & brought to take over cart of Royal Warwicks at LOGEAST WOOD (A 25.b.6.1.) Coys bivouacs at 5pm. 2/Lt J.H.G. Donaldson reported for duty.	
LOGEAST WOOD	26/6/17		Company training during the day.	
	26/6/17		Whole Batn held firing practice on Corps Range.	
	27/6/17		Company training. Bathing at Divisional Baths.	
	28/6/17		Company training. H.B.C. Coys to Div trench working party under A.D.S. 18 2nd Army 2 @ A.28.d.1.7	
	29/6/17		Company training during the day.	
	30/6/17		Company training during the morning. Batn sports during the afternoon.	

Army Form C. 2118.

WAR DIARY
or
INTELLIGENCE SUMMARY.
(Erase heading not required.)

SECRET

WAR DIARY.

2/XIth Batt'n London Regiment.

Volume VI

From :- July 1st 1917.
To :- July 31st 1917.

WAR DIARY
or
INTELLIGENCE SUMMARY.

Army Form C. 2118.

(43) 2/11 London Regt

Place	Date	Hour	Summary of Events and Information	Remarks and references to Appendices
LOG EAST WOOD	July 1/7/17	10.45 am	Church Parade	
		2.30 pm	Brigade Horse Show	
"	2/7/17	4.30 – 12.30	Specialist training	
		10.0 a.m.	N.Coy + 50 O.R.s B. Coy working party at C & 7.5 Parade. 7.0 am. 50 O.R.s B. Coy working party under Lieut the 7 Siege Bty R.M.R.E. at crossing of light Railway and ACHIET-BIHUCOURT road. Found 6.45 am. 50 O.R.s C. Coy working party under Lt. ASIR at A.25 & 17. search 7.0 am. 50 O.R.s C. Coy working party under Maj Siege Bty R.M.R.E. at N°4 9 L.L.S. ACHIET-LE-GRAND. Paraded 6.45 am.	
		2.30 pm	Brigade Round Competition at ACHIET-LE-PETIT CRATER.	
	3rd	8.15 am	General preparation for inspection by G.O.C. 5 & Div.	
		11.30 am	Inspection by Commanding Officer.	
		2.30 pm	Battn Sports.	
		8.0 pm	Battn Concert.	
	4th	9.45 am	Battn paraded for Inspection by G.O.C. Div.	

WAR DIARY or INTELLIGENCE SUMMARY.

Army Form C. 2118.

(4) 2/11 [illegible] Rest

Place	Date	Hour	Summary of Events and Information	Remarks and references to Appendices
LOG EAST WOOD	July 6th	2.30 am	Under O.C. loop arrangements.	[illegible scribble] PJ
"	5th	11.5 pm	Move to BANCOURT.	
BANCOURT bil.	6th	7.0 am	Physical Drill + Bayonet Fighting	
"		2.40	Batt. moved to BERTINCOURT.	
BERTINCOURT	7th July	9.30 – 12.30 and 2.30 – 4.30	O.C. Companies subject to Bathing arrangements. Companies to Inspection of Anti Gas appliances, Ammunition and Emergency Rations.	
"	"	10 a.m.	Company Commanders Commanders Officer + Adjt. reconnoitred Sect. of line to be taken over.	
July 8th 1917			Church parade.	
BERTINCOURT		10.45 am		
		8.45 pm	Batt. proceeded to P.20.947 for entrainment.	
		11.30	Relieved 6th + 7th Manchesters in the left sub-sector Reserve position HAVRINCOURT SECTOR. Relief complete 3.0 am July 9th 1917. Transport lines established at YTRES.	
HAVRINCOURT SECTOR	July 9th 1917	10.0 pm	Working Party 100 O.R. under R.E. digging	

Army Form C. 2118.

WAR DIARY
or
INTELLIGENCE SUMMARY.
(Erase heading not required.)

(45) 2/4 London Regt

Place	Date	Hour	Summary of Events and Information	Remarks and references to Appendices
HAVRINCOURT SECTOR	contd.		digging Northern end of HUBERTS AVENUE	
		11.0 pm	50 O/Rs. under R.E. carrying shelters to front line from FACIT DUMP	
		11.0 pm	60 O/Rs. under R.E. carrying shelters to front line from road K32 c.7.4. Situation Quiet.	
"	July 10/11	9.0 am	50 O/Rs. under R.E. preparation of shelters and drainage in front line.	
"		11.0 pm	50 O/Rs. under R.E. carrying down to front line from FACIT DUMP	
"		11.0 pm	100 O/Rs. under R.E. digging Communication trench (HUBERT'S AVENUE)	
"		11.0 pm	50 O/Rs. under R.E. carrying down to front line from HUBERTS X	
"		9.0 am	25 O/Rs under R.E. preparation of shelters and drainage in front line	
"		10.0 pm	6 O/Rs. under R.E. unloading stores at BROKEN HOUSE DUMP Situation Quiet.	
"	July 11/12	8.30 am	50 O/Rs. under R.E. preparation of shelters in front line.	
"		10.0 pm	25 O/Rs. under R.E. carrying party from BROKEN HOUSE DUMP to front line.	
"		10.30 pm	100 O/Rs. under R.E. digging C.T. HUBERTS AVENUE.	

Army Form C. 2118.

WAR DIARY
or
INTELLIGENCE SUMMARY. (LL) 2/11 London Regt.
(Erase heading not required.)

Place	Date	Hour	Summary of Events and Information	Remarks and references to Appendices
HARGICOURT SECTOR	July 11th	contd. 11.0 pm.	50 o/rs. under R.E. banging party from FACIT DUMP to Front Line.	
"	"	11.0pm	50 o/rs. under R.E. carrying party from ST. HUBERTS PLACE to Front Line. Situation Quiet.	
"	July 12th	9.0 am	25 o/rs. under R.E. water carrying at ST. HUBERTS PLACE	
		10.30pm	100 o/rs. under R.E. deepening F Sup	
		10.30pm	25 o/rs. under R.E. carrying party from MONTMARTE to FRONT LINE	
		10.30pm	100 o/rs. under R.E. digging HUBERTS AVENUE	
		10.30pm	50 o/rs. under R.E. carrying party to FRONT LINE Situation Quiet. — 2 o/rs wounded (D.Coy)	
"	July 13th	9.9 am	25 o/rs under R.E. carrying water ST HUBERTS +	
"		10.30pm	100 o/rs. under R.E. digging F sup.	
"		10.30pm	50 o/rs. under R.E. digging HUBERT AVENUE	
"		10.30pm	50 o/rs. under R.E. carrying stones to FRONT LINE Situation Quiet	

WAR DIARY or INTELLIGENCE SUMMARY

Army Form C. 2118.

(47) 2/11 Lon Regt

Place	Date	Hour	Summary of Events and Information	Remarks and references to Appendices
HAVRINCOURT SECTOR (RESERVE)	July 14.1917	9.0 am	25 ORs under R.E. carrying work ST HUBERTS +	Appx
"	"	9.30 am	50 ORs under R.E. deepening Southern arm of C. Sap.	
"	"	10.30 pm	100 ORs under R.E. deepening tunnel MONTMARTRE	R.E. 9 adj.
"	"	10.30 pm	100 ORs under R.E. digging HUBERTS AVENUE. Situation Quiet.	
"	July 15.1917	9.0 am	25 ORs under R.E. carrying work ST HUBERTS +	Appx
"	"	9.30am-10pm	45 ORs. under RE's fixing up B/C posts & the bridge.	
"	"	10 pm	50 ORs under RE's on drainage of outpost line, near J sap. 11 pm 100 ORs under RE's fixing up E+F posts	
"	"		Situation Quiet.	
"	16/7/17		Inspection of billets by M.O. @ 6pm. Battn relieved the 2/12 Battn Lon left sub sector (front) K.32d.95b5. (5yC HE) & K.26c8010. B Coy on left. C Coy in centre D on right. A in reserve at Q.2.A.4080. Bn HQ Q.2C 8.5. Relief completed by 2.30 am 17/7/17. Casualties 5 ORs wounded	

WAR DIARY

Army Form C. 2118.

(48) 2/11 London Regt

Place	Date	Hour	Summary of Events and Information	Remarks and references to Appendices
HAVRINCOURT LEFT FRONT SUB SECTOR	16/7/17	—	Situation quiet	Wthr fine todays
"	17/7/17	4pm	Situation quiet. Very little artillery activity on either side. Patrols to Bivy frontage nothing to report. No casualties.	Wthr fine todays
"	18/7/17	"	Artillery (enemy) fairly active on front line, especially left Coy front. Bath frontage reduced owing to another Brigade taking over parts of front line. "D" Coy therefore relieved by "B" Coy of 2/10 Bn Ldn Regt, & take over "A" Coy's area Q.2.A.40.80. "A" Coy moving to K.32.C.45.60 to K.32.C.80.40. 1 platoon & 3 platoons to trenches running Q.2.A.48 to K.31.d. (1 OR wounded - at duty)	Wthr fine
"	19/7/17	"	Situation quiet. Enemy artillery fairly active after nightfall. Patrols met no opposition. Casualties 1 OR killed 1 OR wounded	Wthr fine today
"	20/7/17	"	Enemy artillery abnormally active especially on Yorkshire Bank & support line. Enemy aeroplanes active @ 6pm. Casualties 3 ORs wounded. At 10·25pm enemy attempted to raid British post	Wthr not today

T2134. Wt. W708-776. 500000. 4/15. Sir J. C. & S.

WAR DIARY or INTELLIGENCE SUMMARY

Army Form C. 2118.

(49) 2/1 Loyn Regt

Place	Date	Hour	Summary of Events and Information	Remarks and references to Appendices
HAURINE COURT LEFT FRONT SUB-SECTOR	20/7/17	12/Mid	One in 2/10 area between SPUR RD & West side of OXFORD VALLEY. Enemy barrage was heavy but considerable damage to trenches caused several casualties to our garrison. The raid was a failure two prisoners were taken. Enf & 2 enemy Batts on SOS being sent up received telephone orders to reinforce FRONT LINE with 2 Coys in Reserve. At 5 AM 21/4/17 normal dispositions resumed the 2nd Bun on our left were also unsuccessful & received on night of 20/4/17. 8 Lt Pullinger & 10R. wounded. Pte W. Cosplane reported missing was later found to be dying in OUTPOST LINE.	Notes A-l Appx
	21/7/17 22/7/17	6/15 P.m	Situation Quiet. A Coy relieved C Coy in OUTPOST LINE but only with 2 platoons in OUTPOST LINE the other 2 platoons being in FRONT LINE. Relief complete 2.10 AM 22/7/17	Notes Appx
	23/7/17		Situation Quiet. Casualties ord. 9th Battn. carried out successful raid on enemy positions in MON COP. Enemy known to have had 7 killed + 500 wounded. In addition two prisoners were taken	Notes to Appx

WAR DIARY or INTELLIGENCE SUMMARY

Army Form C. 2118.

(50) 2/Lt Foster Res.

Place	Date	Hour	Summary of Events and Information	Remarks and references to Appendices
HAVRINCOURT LEFT FRONT SUB SECTOR	23/4/17	11pm	Situation Quiet. 2/12 Battn raided WIGAN COPSE but it was found to be empty. Casualties suffered by raiding party were, the raiding party came to have killed or wounded 5 officers & 5 ORs & the ID of Underhay & 5 ORs patrols to 100 yds of enemy. 2Lts ID & J Underhay & found enemy line in DEAN COPSE, & found enemy burying	Note re Adj/5
"	24/7/17	11pm	Situation Quiet. 2Lt W F Moors, 2Lt W.J. Underhay & 3 ORs went C.V. diff trenches @ K32 & 65.90 & C10.30 p/m with object of reconnoitring RAVINE. Patrol was fired on several times & had to return @ 11pm owing to hostile patrols. Patrol went out again at 2:30am, went again & fired on the reconnoitred to northern Y5 yds DEAN COPSE. Owing to daylight, patrol returned @ 4AM. Casualties Nil. Went W/H Kennels & 3 ORs reconnoitred YORKSHIRE BANK. CASUALTIES Nil	Note re Adj.
"	25/7/17		Situation Quiet. 2/Lt Underhay & 2/Lt Moore went out with Fighting Patrol of 20 ORs from K32 C65.90, met with opposition about to gain an identification the enemy retired again, during our 16 hours Casualties Nil	Note re-1 Adj—
"	26/7/17 27/7/17	7	Situation Quiet. Relief Carried. Battn arrived @ 10.15 & 1/5 Battn Q.O. Canadians. Relief Complete @ 12.40 AM. 1/5 Battn in relief entrained 22/15	Note Adj/6

Army Form C. 2118.

WAR DIARY
or
INTELLIGENCE SUMMARY. (51) 2/11 Batts Lon Regt.
(Erase heading not required.)

Instructions regarding War Diaries and Intelligence Summaries are contained in F. S. Regs., Part II. and the Staff Manual respectively. Title pages will be prepared in manuscript.

Place	Date	Hour	Summary of Events and Information	Remarks and references to Appendices
HAVRINCOURT LEFT FRONT SUB SECTOR	26/1/19 27/1/19		At HUBERTS CROSS Q.76.97 on light Railway - proceeded to CAMP @ RUYAULCOURT, resting until 4pm.	
	27/1/19	4pm	Batn entrained on light railway @ 4pm for BAPAUME arriving 1 AM 28/1/19. Then Batn entrained at BRIGADE sidings from Gare BEAUMETZ arriving @ 5 PM. Batn then marched to WARLUS, occupying billets this Day	
WARLUS	29/1/19		Spent in cleaning up. Church Parade 11 AM.	
"	30/1/19 31/1/19		} Cleaning up & refitting men	

Army Form C. 2118.

WAR DIARY
or
INTELLIGENCE SUMMARY.

(Erase heading not required.)

SECRET

War Diary
2/11 Batts London Regt

From 1st August 1917
to 31st " " Volume 7.

WAR DIARY
INTELLIGENCE SUMMARY.
(Erase heading not required.)

Army Form C. 2118.

(52) 2/11 Batts London Regt

Place	Date	Hour	Summary of Events and Information	Remarks and references to Appendices
WARLUS	1/8/17	10pm	Inquisitive move, carried 7 platoon training carried on with. Draft of 93 riflemen reported to Battn 3/4/17.	
"	2/8/17	10am	Platoon training	
"	3/8/17		Platoon training & bathing at Dainville	
"	4/8/17		Platoon training	
"	5/8/17		Battn Church parade.	
"	6/8/17		Platoon training	
"	7/8/17		Platoon " Battn Sports during afternoon	
"	8/8/17		Brigade Practice attack at WAILLY TRENCHES	
"	9/8/17		Platoon training during morning Battn Sports in afternoon	
"	10/8/17		Brigade assault at arms sports at aerodrome, DAINVILLE	
"	11/8/17		Company training Bathing during the day	
"	12/8/17			

WAR DIARY
or
INTELLIGENCE SUMMARY.

Army Form C. 2118.

(53) 2/11 Bn John Regt.

Place	Date	Hour	Summary of Events and Information	Remarks and references to Appendices
WARLUS	13/8/17	10.a.	Platoon & Company Training.	*note to issue*
"	14/8/17	"	— Do —	*note re issue*
"	15/8/17	"	Brigade practice attack at Wally Trenches	*note w/issue*
"	16/8/17	"	Battn practice attack at Wally Trenches	
"	17/8/17	"	Platoon training & Bathing	
"	18/8/17	"	— do —	
"	19/8/17	"	Church Parade	
"	20/8/17	"	Company Training. Coys on Range at WANQUETIN	*note*
"	21/8/17	"	Divisional practice attack at Wally. Warning Order received from Brigade of the Division being transferred from 3rd Army to 5th Army.	*to? Adjt*
"	22/8/17	"	Company Training. Coys on Range at WANQUETIN	
"	23/8/17	"	— do — "A" Coy moved to ARRAS to act as	

Army Form C. 2118.

(54) 2/11 Br Cam Regt

WAR DIARY
or
INTELLIGENCE SUMMARY.
(Erase heading not required.)

Instructions regarding War Diaries and Intelligence Summaries are contained in F. S. Regs., Part II. and the Staff Manual respectively. Title pages will be prepared in manuscript.

Place	Date	Hour	Summary of Events and Information	Remarks and references to Appendices
WARLUS	23/8/17	10pm	As loading party to Brigade Group (Strength: 5 officers 190 OR's) 1 Battn for night at Arras, reporting to RTO Arras @ 3.24 AM 24/8/17.	
"	24/8/17	3 pm	Battn (less A Coy) marched to Arras Station & entrained @ 6.50 pm for PROVEN, arriving 5 AM 25/8/17	
"	25/8/17	10 pm	Marched from PROVEN to BRAKE Camp situated @ fort Roads 1 mile NW of the V in VLAMERTINGHE. Battn in XVIII Corps 5th Army	
BRAKE CAMP	26/8/17	"	Day spent in cleaning up & reconnoitering dirs at St JURIEN	
"	27/8/17		Battn moved to RAIGESBURG Camp H 6 b @ 9 pm. Transport lines remained at BRAKE Camp move to Potter Farm on 29/8/17	
RAIGESBURG CAMP	28/8/17	"	Battn moved up the line to relieve 5th [?] regt in dug outs on East West support lane 2/10 Battn 5th regt	
YSER CANAL BANK	29/8/17		of YSER Canal Bank at I.16 + C.25 d (28 N.W.2) (Ed 6m). 2/10 Battn Can Regt.	

Quiet day. Very little artillery activity except

Army Form C. 2118.

WAR DIARY
or
INTELLIGENCE SUMMARY.

(53) 2/4 Batt. Lon Regt

(Erase heading not required.)

Instructions regarding War Diaries and Intelligence Summaries are contained in F. S. Regs., Part II. and the Staff Manual respectively. Title pages will be prepared in manuscript.

Place	Date	Hour	Summary of Events and Information	Remarks and references to Appendices
YSER CANAL BANKS	30/9/17	10pm	Quiet day. Situation normal	H/Wilkie Capt & Adjt
"	31/9/17	12 noon	Quiet day - do -	Moore Lieut & adjt

Army Form C. 2118.

WAR DIARY
or
INTELLIGENCE SUMMARY.
(Erase heading not required.)

175/58

Vol 9

SECRET.

WAR DIARY

2nd 2/XI th Bn. London Regt.

From:- 1st September, 1917.
To:- 30th September, 1917.

WAR DIARY or INTELLIGENCE SUMMARY.

(56) 2/11 Batn Lon Regt

Army Form C. 2118.

Place	Date	Hour	Summary of Events and Information	Remarks and references to Appendices
YSER CANAL	1/9/17	7pm	Batn moved to relieve 2/10 Batn Lon Regt in Outpost-line. 'B' Coys in outposts 'C' on left in Springfield posts 'B' on right. 'D' Coy in support in St Julien. 'A' in Reserve in CALIFORNIA DRIVE. Batn HQ C.12.C.12. Relief completed @ 11pm. Casualties 3 ORs wounded	Wise Capt & adjt
ST JULIEN	2/9/17	11pm	Situation Quiet. Line of STEENBEEK & neighbourhood of Bn. HQ shelled. Casualties 3 ORs wounded	Wise Capt & adjt
"	3/9/17	"	Hostile artillery very active. Heavy barrages put down on STEENBEEK. At 9pm 2nd Lt O.G. King & 40 ORs of 'C' Coy left SPRINGFIELD to capture & hold SPOT FARM. This was found to be unoccupied. Position was consolidated & added to Batns Outpost Line. Casualties 6 killed & 10 wounded (ORs). Situation Quiet. Two ORs killed & 4 wounded	Wise Capt & adjt
"	4/9/17	"	"	Wise Capt & adjt
"	5/9/17	"	During the evening heavy hostile artillery activity. Batn relieved in line by 2/9 Batn Lon Regt	Capt & adjt

Army Form C. 2118.

WAR DIARY
or
INTELLIGENCE SUMMARY.
(Erase heading not required.)

(54) 2/11 Battn London Regt

Place	Date	Hour	Summary of Events and Information	Remarks and references to Appendices
St Julien	5/9/17		Took over positions in Res. on East West Bank of	Whole copies appx
	6/9/17		YSER CANAL. Casualties 1 killed 4 wounded	
YSER CANAL		2pm	Battn. moved from Canal being relieved by 2/12, & proceeded to DEMBRE CAMP (B27c.86)	Whole copies appx
DEMBRE CAMP	7/9/17	10pm	Day spent in cleaning up, bathing at Dureosoul Baths.	Whole copies appx
	8/9/17		Platoon training. At 1.15 AM Enemy Aircraft dropped bombs in Transport lines, killing 13 horses & wounding 7 horses.	Whole copies appx
	9/9/17		Platoon training	Whole copies appx
	10/9/17		- do -	Whole copies appx
	11/9/17	9am	Battn moved from DEMBRE CAMP & took over BRAKE CAMP (A30 central)	Whole copies appx
BRAKE CAMP	12/9/17		Platoon training	Whole copies appx

Army Form C. 2118.

WAR DIARY
or
INTELLIGENCE SUMMARY. (58) 2/11 Battn London Regt
(Erase heading not required.)

Instructions regarding War Diaries and Intelligence Summaries are contained in F. S. Regs., Part II. and the Staff Manual respectively. Title pages will be prepared in manuscript.

Place	Date	Hour	Summary of Events and Information	Remarks and references to Appendices
BRAKE CAMP	13/9/17	10pm	Platoon training	Those capt edge
"	14/9/17		- do -	Those capt edge
"	15/9/17		- do - 150 ORs working party under PC at SIEGE CAMP	Those capt edge
"	16/9/17		B2yA 28. Two ORs wounded by splinters from hostile aircraft. Divine Service - 150 ORs working party under PC at SIEGE CAMP B2yA 28 - 2 platoons at 58th Div HQ.	Those capt edge
"	17/9/17		Company training on area A 28 b 29. All days firing on range	Those capt edge
"	18/9/17		Company training - do -	Those capt edge
"	19/9/17			Those capt edge
"	20/9/17	3AM	Battn moved from BRAKE CAMP Honeveaux to to CAMP, REIGERSBURG. Recvd unnumbered orders of GOC 174th Brigade for the Divisional attack. At 8.45 AM orders issued for Battn to move to CALIFORNIA DRIVE	Those capt edge

A 5834 Wt. W 4973/M687 750,000 8/16 D. D. & L. Ltd. Forms/C.2118/13.

WAR DIARY or INTELLIGENCE SUMMARY

Army Form C. 2118.

(59) 2/4 Batt. Lon. Regt.

Place	Date	Hour	Summary of Events and Information	Remarks and references to Appendices
	20/9/17	—	Telk. over from 2/4 London Regt. who had moved forward to Mon du Hibou as visits any zenny counter attack. Continuous artillery fire during the day. Night's 4 am Divc. expresses some period.	Major / Capt. Adjt.
S. of ST JEAN ST JULIEN	21/9/17	—	10.5 A.M. Orders received from G.O.C. 174th to Major C.W.D. Boys to Mon du Hibou Area, to counter attack if necessary at E & W Lun or C & G Nouveau points to move to ARBRE & HUBNER FARM. Whering to break off any counter attack that his one not necessary. Div H.Q. were also received from 173rd Brigade for the Batt. to relieve posts of 174th & 173rd Inf. Brigades on fronts held during the evening until 2/10 Batt. London Regt. on left A Coy. relieved in WINNIPEG AREA "B" Coy and WURST FARM AREA "C" Coy. VON TIRPITZ FARM & CLIFTON HOUSE AREA. Batt. H.Q. - JOLET FARM Casualties 1 O.R.	Major / Capt. Adjt.
JOLET FARM ST JULIEN	22/9/17	—	Enemy Artillery Heavily Active. Casualties O.R.'s 10 of whom wounded & Kd. A Batts. wounded and at duty. Mr. H Wilkers & Parented.	Major / Capt. Adjt.
	23/9/17	—	Enemy's Artillery more very Active. SOS sent up on left sector	GOC / Adjt.

Army Form C. 2118.

WAR DIARY or INTELLIGENCE SUMMARY.
(Erase heading not required.)

(60) 2/1 Battn Lon Regt.

Place	Date	Hour	Summary of Events and Information	Remarks and references to Appendices
YPRES SALIENT	26/9/17	—	@ 9am. 2 enemy runners arrived which was beaten off. 2Lt. J.R. Mason wounded. ORs. 10 killed & 38 wounded. Capt. AS Sowton ordered to form one of the 60th Regt. Suy Standard.	Mothe Capt AS Sowton
"	26/9/17	—	Situation quiet. 2/Lt A. Parker killed in action. ORs 2 killed & 14 wounded. 2/Lt SmQ Ford wounded at duty.	Mothe 2Lts Parker
"	25/9/17	—	Situation quiet. Battn relieved in the line by 2/2 & 2/9 Battns London Regt. who were forming up on the Cluster Houses – Schuler Farm Jct. Relief was down 5.40 am. 26/9. Relief completed @ 11.30 pm 25/9. Casualties 2 killed & 2 ORs wounded. Battn on relief took over trenches EAST BANK OF CANAL. 2 Lt Symonds wounded at duty. Brigade attack successful.	Mothe Capt O/Coff
"	27/9/17 8.30 am		Battn moved from Canal Bank to DAMBRE CAMP	Mothe Capt O/Coff
DAMBRE CAMP	28/9/17	—	Company Training. Drafts of 5 officers & 249 ORs arrived from Depot Battn.	Mothe Capt O/Coff
"	29/9/17	"	Company Training. Horse arrange dropped bombs in vicinity of camp. Casualties 2 ORs wounded.	Mothe Capt O/Coff

Army Form C. 2118.

WAR DIARY
or
INTELLIGENCE SUMMARY. (61) 2/11 Battn Lon Regt

(Erase heading not required.)

Place	Date	Hour	Summary of Events and Information	Remarks and references to Appendices
Dambre Camp	30/9/17	9.45 am	Battn moved from Dambre Camp to Brake Camp A 30 Central	Morale report C2/17

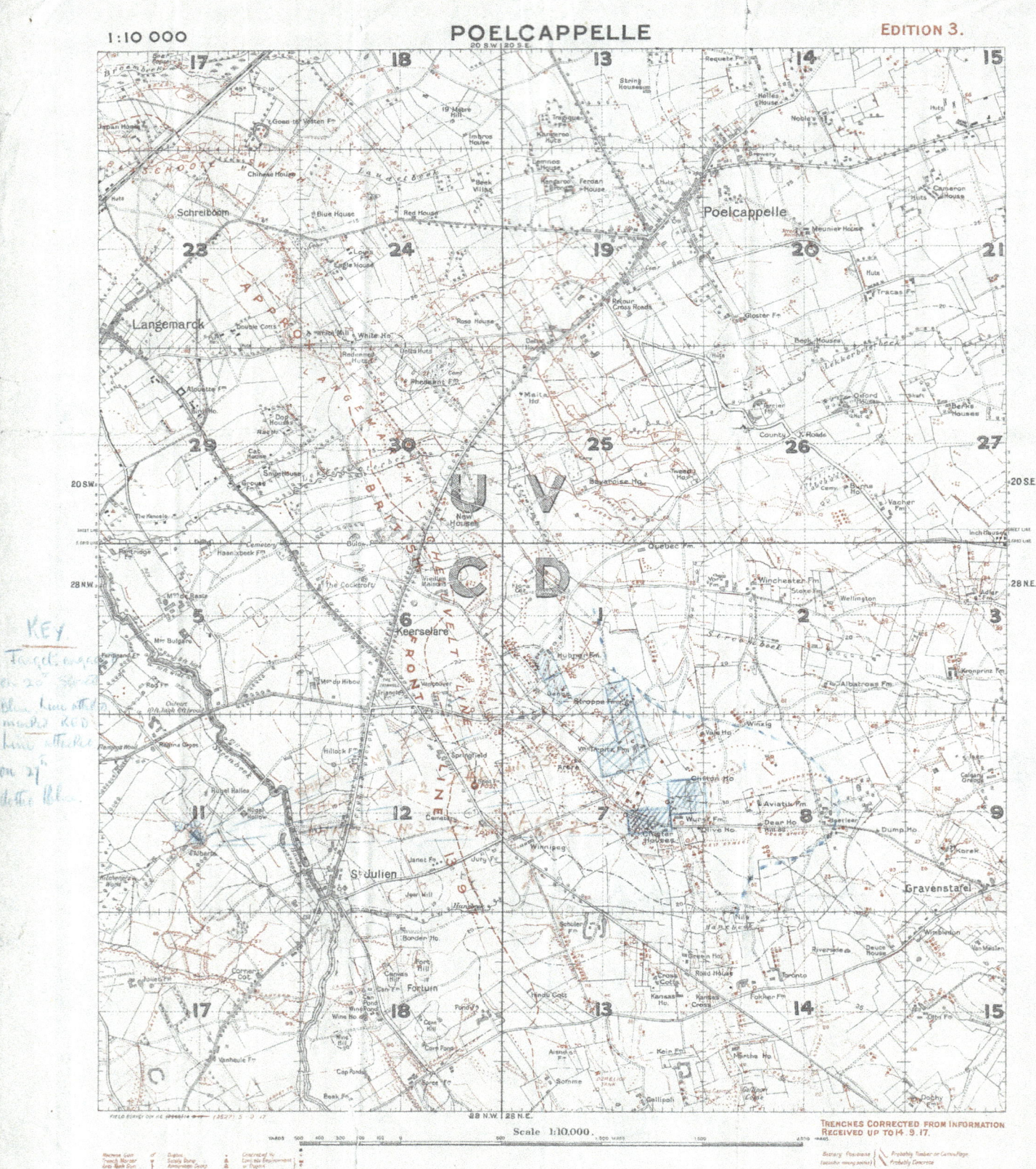

15

Vol 10

Confidential

War Diary – Volume I

2/11th Bn. London Regt.

October 1917.

Army Form C. 2118.

WAR DIARY
INTELLIGENCE SUMMARY.
(Erase heading not required.)

(62) 2/11 Batt. Kings Regt.

Place	Date	Hour	Summary of Events and Information	Remarks and references to Appendices
BRAKE CAMP	1/10/17	12 NOON	Batt. moved from BRAKE CAMP to entrain @ VLAMERTINGHE. Nos. entrained 18 officers 790 O.R. Arrived AUDRUQUES at 12 MIDNIGHT & marched to billets at RECQUES.	Mottle Capt. & Adjt
"	2/10/17		Day spent in bathing cleaning up. 2/Lt. W Ferris awarded MC	Mottle
RECQUES	3/10/17	10.5 am	Company Training. 2/Lt. R.S. Gaun reported for duty.	Mottle
"	4/10/17	"	7 officers & 390 O.Rs. proceeded to CASSALS for the day. by Coys. Uns & lorry. Bn of Coys - bombs throwing. Company training, specialists classes. 2/Lt O.S. King awarded M.C	Mottle Capt & Adjt
"	5/10/17	"	Company training, specialists Classes - do -	Mottle Capt & Adjt
"	6/10/17	"	Church parade.	Mottle Capt & Adjt
"	7/10/17	"	Company training specialists Classes Quiet ferring at GUEMY - do -	Mottle Capt & Adjt
"	8/10/17	"	do Capt. W.R. Smith awarded M.C.	Mottle Capt & Adjt

Army Form C. 2118.

WAR DIARY
INTELLIGENCE SUMMARY.
(Erase heading not required.)

(63) 2/11 Batt. Can Rest

Place	Date	Hour	Summary of Events and Information	Remarks and references to Appendices
RECQUES	10/10/17	10am	Company & Specialist training.	Whole Capt.
"	11/10/17	"	-do- Brigade Tactical scheme for Officers	Whole Capt. Coy.
"	12/10/17	"	Bath on "B" RANGE	Whole Capt. Coy.
"	13/10/17	"	Company training	Whole Capt. Coy.
"	14/10/17	"	Inspection of Bath by OC	Whole Capt. Coy.
"	15/10/17	"	Brigade Tactical exercise	Whole Capt. Adv.
"	16/10/17	"	Battalion Drill & Company training.	Whole Capt. Adv.
"	17/10/17	"	Brigade Inspection & presentation of awards by GOC 19 Division	Whole Capt's Adv.
"	18/10/17	"	Bathing during the morning, Bath'n tactical attack on "B" area during the afternoon. Drafts of 41 ORs reported	Whole Capt "B" area
"	19/10/17	"	Bath'n Brigade in the attack practise on "B" area	Whole Capt. Coy.

Army Form C. 2118.

WAR DIARY
or
INTELLIGENCE SUMMARY.
(Erase heading not required.)

(64) 2/4 Lon Regt

Instructions regarding War Diaries and Intelligence Summaries are contained in F. S. Regs., Part II. and the Staff Manual respectively. Title pages will be prepared in manuscript.

Place	Date	Hour	Summary of Events and Information	Remarks and references to Appendices
RECQUES	21/10/17	10 pm	Company training during the day.	Yhole Capt & adjt
"	22/10/17	10.15 am	Battn moved to St Janter Biezen Area (Road Camp) entraining at Audriques for Hopoutre at 1 pm detraining 4 pm, then marched to Road Camp (F25d 42 Sheet 27 NE) 27 officers & 741 ORs.	Yhole Capt - S Engr
ROAD CAMP	22/10/17	10 pm	Day spent in cleaning up &c.	Yhole Capt - Adjt
"	23/10/17	"	Company training	Yhole Capt - Adjt
"	24/10/17	"	Brigade Practice attack in training area & specialist classes	Yhole Capt - Adjt
"	25/10/17	"	Platoon boy training	Yhole Capt - Adjt
"	26/10/17	"	CO's - CO, OC Coys, TO Lers Officer & IO reconnoitred front line	Yhole Capt - Adjt
"	27/10/17	"	Platoon boy training	Yhole Capt - Adjt

A 5834 Wt. W4973/M687 750,000 8/16 D. D. & L. Ltd. Forms/C.2118/13.

Army Form C. 2118

WAR DIARY
INTELLIGENCE SUMMARY

(Erase heading not required.)

(65) 2/11 London Regt

Instructions regarding War Diaries and Intelligence Summaries are contained in F.S. Regs., Part II. and the Staff Manual respectively. Title Pages will be prepared in manuscript.

Place	Date	Hour	Summary of Events and Information	Remarks and references to Appendices
ROAD CAMP	22/10/17	10 am	Church Service	Appx "A" Coln. Ops. Orders Appx "B" Copy Opps.
"	29/10/17		Platoon & Coy training. Other practise in B Area.	Appx "C" Coln. Orders
"	30/10/17		Batln moved from Road Camp to Siege Camp entraining at RAIKHOER at 1.5 pm & detraining at BRIGEN. Thence march to SIEGE CAMP	
SIEGE CAMP	3/11/17	2.30 pm	Batn moved from Siege Camp to Camp Bank.	Appx "D" Coln. Ops. Orders

Lewinton
Major
a/o.c. 2/11 London Regt.

1875 Wt. W593/826 1,000,000 4/15 J.B.C. & A. A.D.S.S./Forms/C. 2118.

Army Form C. 2118

WAR DIARY
~~INTELLIGENCE SUMMARY~~
(Erase heading not required.)

Vol. 11

SECRET.

WAR DIARY.

2/XIth Bn. LONDON REGT.

From:- 1st November 1917
To:- 31st November 1917

Army Form C. 2118.

WAR DIARY
or
INTELLIGENCE SUMMARY.
(Erase heading not required.)

(66) 2/11 Batt London Regt

Place	Date	Hour	Summary of Events and Information	Remarks and references to Appendices
YSER CANAL BANK	1/11/17	10am	Day spent in clearing up quarters. 12 noon "D" Coy moved to KEMPTON PARK, taking over from 1 Coy of 2/12 in Reserve. "D" Coy found working party of 1 officer & 100 O.Rs under R.Es carrying duckboards from CHESTER FARM its TRACKS. Casualties 2 O.R. wounded	J.H.Hope Capt. & Adjt
"	2/11/17	2.30 p.m.	H.Qs, A & C Coys moved to KEMPTON PARK in Reserve taking over from 2/12 Lon Regt. "B" Coy moved to PHEASANT TRENCH in Support relieving one Coy of 2/10. A & C Coys found working party of 2 officers & 150 ORs carrying duckboards under R.Es. Casualties 2 ORs wounded. 1 gassed.	J.H.Hope Capt. & Adjt
KEMPTON PARK	3/11/17	10am	Day spent in reconnoitering lines. Lt Col WH Symonds wounded. Capt A.fe. Eve CdeG Dallas Payne attached 2/11 wounded 1 OR killed & 1 wounded	J.H.Hope Capt. & Adjt
"	4/11/17	2.30 p.m.	Battn relieved 2/12 in the line. Dispositions, A Coy Two Nobles Farm & Platoon posts. Dispositions of "D" in Res at BREWERY. "B" Coy in PLATOON POSTS in CENTRE at MEUNIER Hd POEDAPELLE	J.H.Hope Capt. & Adjt

Army Form C. 2118.

WAR DIARY
or
INTELLIGENCE SUMMARY. (Erase heading not required.)

(64) 2/1 Batt. London Regt.

Place	Date	Hour	Summary of Events and Information	Remarks and references to Appendices
	4/11/17		10 Coys on right in platoon posts at Trenchy Farm & 2 platoons of B Coy in Reserve at Egoster Farm. Relief complete 11.45 p.m. Enemy barrage observed relief. Heavy barrage put down from 4.45 to 5.15 p.m. Casualties to noon 5/11/17 O.R.'s killed 18 wounded & 2 missing	Afford Capt's copy Copy-0 copy
POELCAPELLE	5/11/17 10 p.m.		Hostile artillery quiet. 3 O.R.'s wounded	Afford Capt's copy
"	6/11/17		Heavy hostile barrage put down from 6.54 am to 12 noon. Gradually decreasing in answer to Canadians attack on right. 2/10 Bn London Regt relieved Batt in the line during the night, relief being completed at 1.30 am 7/11/17. Batt on relief proceeded to Kempton Park & embussed for Siege Camp – no 5. Casualties to noon 7/11 – 3 O.R.'s killed 11 O.R.'s wounded	Afford Capt's copy
SIEGE CAMP	7/11/17		Day spent in resting cleaning up	Afford Capt's copy
"	8/11/17		– do –	

WAR DIARY
INTELLIGENCE SUMMARY

Army Form C. 2118

(68) 2/1 Battn Lon Regt.

Place	Date	Hour	Summary of Events and Information	Remarks and references to Appendices
SIEGE CAMP	9/11/17	10 pm	Company & Specialist training	
"	10/11/17	"	- do -	
"	11/11/17	"	Church Parade. Company - Specialist training	
"	12/11/17	"	- do -	
"	13/11/17	"	- do -	
"	14/11/17	1.20 pm	Battn moved from SIEGE CAMP to DIVISIONAL CENTRAL CAMP, PROVEN (F.76.52) entraining at ELVERDINGHE STATION @ 2.30 pm, detraining at PROVEN. Transport by road.	
PROVEN	15/11/17	10 pm	Day spent in cleaning up. 2/Lt Loder & 105 ORs & 4 officers, all Batto surplus reported from Div Depot Battn	
"	16/11/17	10 pm	Company & Specialist training	
"	17/11/17	"	- do -	
"	18/11/17	"	Church parade. Bathing. Company & Specialist training	
"	19/11/17	"		

WAR DIARY or INTELLIGENCE SUMMARY

Army Form C. 2118.

(69) 2/11 Batts [London] Regt.

Hour, Date, Place	Summary of Events and Information	Remarks and references to Appendices
10pm 20/11/17 PROVEN	Company Specialist Training	Strobe Cost-rolle
21/11/17 "	- Do -	Strutt Bopk & Corp
22/11/17 "	- Do -	Sproxh Special
23/11/17 "	- Do -	Thursday (Saturday)
24/11/17 "	Church Parade in Cinema Hut Proven. Bathing.	Thursday (Saturday) Thursday (Saturday)
25/11/17 "	Company at Specialist Training. Draper proceeded by road to ST. MOMELIN.	
26/11/17 "	Company Specialist Training. Advance Party proceeded by road from ST.	Sunday Sunday
27/11/17 "	MOMELIN to SENINGHEM. Batt. entrained at PROVEN at 12.0 noon	Thursday (Saturday)

Army Form C. 2118.

WAR DIARY
or
INTELLIGENCE SUMMARY
(Erase heading not required.)

Hour, Date, Place	Summary of Events and Information	Remarks and references to Appendices
Nov 27th 1917 PROVEN	Arrived WIZERNES at 2.0 pm but as ordered by rail march 1st guide to SENINGHEM.	[illegible signature]
W 28th SENINGHEM	General rearrangement of billets and cleaning up — Inspection of Works by C.O. in week — Inspection of billets.	[illegible signature] [illegible signature]
Th 29th 1917 9 am — 12pm SENINGHEM	Squad Section & Company training March Discipline — Musketry — Ordres — Bayonet fighting. Riding class.	[illegible signature]
Fri 30th 9.0 — 12.0 pm SENINGHEM	Squad Section & Company training March Discipline — Musketry — close order drill — Bayonet fighting — Lewis Gunners. — Rifle for selected — Officer Riding class	[illegible signature] [illegible signatures]

CONFIDENTIAL.

Headquarters,
 58th Division. (Advanced)

    Herewith War Diary of the 2/11th London Regt., which was returned for signature, as explained in my B.M.F. 21/6 of November 6th.

    The delay is much regretted.

8th November 1917.

BRIGADIER-GENERAL,
CMDG 175th INFANTRY BDE.

Army Form C. 2118.

Vol 12

WAR DIARY
or
INTELLIGENCE SUMMARY.
(Erase heading not required.)

Confidential

War Diary
2/11 London Regt

from Dec 1st 1917
31st 1917

Army Form C. 2118.

WAR DIARY
or
INTELLIGENCE SUMMARY

(Erase heading not required.)

(71) 2/4th York & Lancs Regt

Instructions regarding War Diaries and Intelligence Summaries are contained in F.S. Regs, Part II. and the Staff Manual respectively. Title pages will be prepared in manuscript.

Hour, Date, Place	Summary of Events and Information	Remarks and references to Appendices
Dec 1st 1917 SENINGHEM	9.0 am } March Discipline – Musketry – Arms and Clothes – order drills – Bayonet 1pm } fighting – Outpost duties – Intelligence duties. Afternoon – Sports and Officers Riding class	G. Lindsay Lieut/Adjt
Dec 2nd 1917 SENINGHEM	Voluntary Church Service in the Cue School SENINGHEM at 8 & 7.30 am 9.0 am and 5.30 pm. Brigade Conference at 11 am	G. Lindsay Lieut/Adjt
Dec 3rd 1917 SENINGHEM	9.0 am } Coy Musketry in camp – recruits to } sections drill – Lewis Machine drill 1.0 pm } – Musketry and March Discipline Afternoon – Sports and Officers Riding class	G. Lindsay Lieut/Adjt

Army Form C. 2118.

WAR DIARY
or
INTELLIGENCE SUMMARY (92) 2/11 Ldn Regt
(Erase heading not required.)

Instructions regarding War Diaries and Intelligence Summaries are contained in F. S. Regs, Part II. and the Staff Manual respectively. Title pages will be prepared in manuscript.

Hour, Date, Place	Summary of Events and Information	Remarks and references to Appendices
December 4th 1917 BEMINGHEM	9 am 1 pm } B Coy on Range remember Salving ammunition and monthly returns close are due. Afternoon Games and Officers Riding lessons	[signature] Lieut. Col.
December 5th 1917	9.0 am - 1.0 pm } Companies at disposal of OsC Companies for inspection of arms, appearance, gas drill, foot inspection, Kit inspection, cleaning equipment and towels in the meantime. 6, breaking in Lewis Gunners. Afternoon Games	[signature] Lieut. Col.
Dec 6th 1917	6.0 am Battn marched to rendezvous on main CHERIS road and entrained at 6.0 am and proceeded to WIZERNES. Luncheon at WIZERNES and arrived at ELVERDINGHE Station at about 2.0 pm. Marched to No 5 Camp SIEGE Camps.	[signature] Lieut. Col.

Army Form C. 2118.

(73) 1/4 Loan Regt

WAR DIARY
or
INTELLIGENCE SUMMARY

(Erase heading not required.)

Hour, Date, Place	Summary of Events and Information	Remarks and references to Appendices
Brandhoek Camp continued	Inniskn SIEGE Camp - Nos much altered and allowed to rest for remainder of day.	[signature] Lieutenant Commanding
SIEGE CAMP Dec 9th 1917	S.O. 2ndLt Fay commanded out I.O. reconnoitred position in the air and made arrangements with operator for taking over in the line. Companies stood ordered etc. in vicinity of camp.	[signature] Lieutenant Commanding
SIEGE CAMP Dec 10 1917	12 noon moved off from SIEGE CAMP E BATTDS CAUSEWAY. HOTEL. Stores sent to Rats. 2.30 (Batln with HQ guides (1 per platoon 1 per Coy) HdQrs 2 Bn HQr) and proceeded to take over the left subsector (POELCAPEL Sector) from 16R Shropshire Inranted. Relief completed 6.45p. Sentries issued from REQUETTE FARM to the right. E in B COMPANIES on the left. C Coy right front D Coy left front A Coy in support +B Coy. Lewis Contd. Attach Company.	[signature] Lieutenant Commanding

1247 W 3299 200,000 (E) 8/14 J.B.C. & A. Forms/C. 2118/11.

Army Form C. 2118.

WAR DIARY
or
INTELLIGENCE SUMMARY

(Erase heading not required.)

(4th) 2/11 Lond Regt

Instructions regarding War Diaries and Intelligence Summaries are contained in F. S. Regs., Part II. and the Staff Manual respectively. Title pages will be prepared in manuscript.

Hour, Date, Place	Summary of Events and Information	Remarks and references to Appendices
Left Sub Section POEL C & PE L Section Dec. 9th 1917.	Quiet night – very little shelling. Quiet day – few enemy shells on neighbouring trenches during evening. Casualties nil.	St Winnebeek Jan 9th 1917
Dec 10th 1917	Quiet day and night – boundary shelling. Fresh enemy no shelling of front trenches.	St Winnebeek Jan 10th 1917
Dec 11th 1917	Quiet day. Bath reliefs in from line by 2/X in both London Regt. Relief complete 9.0 pm. Battalion in support. Battn H.Q. D. left in EAGLE Trench. B Coy in CANDLE Trench. H. Qrs. at DOUBLE COTTS.	St Winnebeek Jan 11th 1917
Left Sub Section Support Section Dec 12th 1917	Quiet day spent in improving accommodation and dugouts – slight few shelling during early evening.	St Winnebeek Jan 12th 1917

Army Form C. 2118.

(15) 4th Lon Regt

WAR DIARY
or
INTELLIGENCE SUMMARY.
(Erase heading not required.)

Place	Date	Hour	Summary of Events and Information	Remarks and references to Appendices
Left Sub Sector			Quiet day spent in intermittent reconnaissance and drainage of Support position trenches. B to A Coy moved back to CANDLE TRENCH. Reinforcements to remaining coys received in integument.	St Quentin fragment
Left Sub sector	Dec 11th 1917		EAGLE trench heavily bombarded from 7.0 am to 1.0 pm. Casualties 2 O/Rs D Coy. Bn relieving the 7/8 Mdx from London Regt in the forward position. Relief complete 8.15 pm. Dispositions others in frontage line a three company one. Right Coy B Coy, Centre Coy A Coy, Left Coy D Coy, loose centre trench coy C Coy.	St Quentin fragment
Left Sub sector forward position	Dec 15th 1917		Quiet night. All posts manned throughout and work continued on new mini wire line of L Coy & R.3. Persons brought in from REQUETTE FARM (B Coy) during night of 15th. Casualties 1 O/R slightly wounded.	St Quentin fragment

A.834 Wt.W4973/M687 750,000 8/16 D.D.&L.Ltd. Forms/C.2118/13.

Army Form C. 2118.

WAR DIARY
or
INTELLIGENCE SUMMARY.
(Erase heading not required.)

(96) 2/11 Lon Regt.

Place	Date	Hour	Summary of Events and Information	Remarks and references to Appendices
Left sub Sector Forward position	Dec 16th 1917		Quiet night (15th) Considerable numbers will help of R.E. Infantry and transport all sorts, cleaning out trenches etc. Batt relieved in the line by 1/23rd Batt London Regt. Relief complete 7.25 p.m. Some (four) O.Rs slightly wounded & Lieut. W.H. Smith slightly wounded. 2 O.Rs report wounded. On relief Coy proceeded to BATTLE (500'S.T. KEMPTON PARK) and moved to Ft READING (vicinity of ELVERDINGHE) and onwards to route march thence to WHITE MILL CAMP (Sunny arriving in huts his 29 O/rs and horses to "Surplice" crews & trans. feed)	Appendix Summary
BRIDGE WHITE MILL CAMP	Dec 17 & 18 17		Day spent in resting and cleaning up kit — working of fell out. Reinforcements will to arrive — hand foot preparation	Appendix Summary

Army Form C. 2118.

WAR DIARY
or
INTELLIGENCE SUMMARY. (77) 2/11 London Regt.
(Erase heading not required.)

Place	Date	Hour	Summary of Events and Information	Remarks and references to Appendices
BRIDGE CAMP	18/7/17	10am.	Company Training loading	Bright. Capt? page Nath. Cas: as
"	19/7/17	"	Do.	
"	20/7/17	"	Do.	
"	21/7/17	"	Do.	
"	22/7/17	"	Do.	Fine
"	23/7/17	"	Church parade. Memorial service for Officers NCO's & men killed in action at Divnl Army Sport. begn Camp 10.30am.	Capt: as

WAR DIARY
or
INTELLIGENCE SUMMARY. (78) 2/11 London Regt

Army Form C. 2118.

Place	Date	Hour	Summary of Events and Information	Remarks and references to Appendices
BRIDGE CAMP	24/9/17	10.55 p.m.	Battn moved from Bridge Camp to relieve 2/3 London Regt in support in left sub. sector (Bellecourt). DAC Coy in Eagle Trench B. Coy in Candle Trench. Battn HQ Double Copse. No casualties. Relief complete 5 a.m.	
LEFT SUB SECTOR BELLECOURT SUPPORT	25/9/17		Hostile artillery fairly active. Considerable work done in Eagle Trench. No casualties.	
"	26/9/17		Quiet day. No casualties.	
"	27/9/17		3 OR wounded.	
"	28/9/17	5pm	Battn moved from support to relieve 2/10 London Regt in front line. Disposition D Coy on right at Tausse & Berthier A in centre at Seneark & pos B on right at Ferdi HQ & posts. 16 counter attacking Coy at Obgate 1602. Relief complete 4.45 am Casualties Nil.	

Army Form C. 2118.

WAR DIARY
or
INTELLIGENCE SUMMARY. (79) 2/4 Bolton Regt
(Erase heading not required.)

Place	Date	Hour	Summary of Events and Information	Remarks and references to Appendices
LEFT SUB SECTOR PONT PERLE	30/12/17	10 pm	Quiet day. Improving posts using barbed wire during the night. 142nd Brigade on left attacked German front line at COLIBRI FARM, TURENNE CROSSING V.1.C.8.0, & forming up west of our posts at BERTHIER. Attack launched up on right. Slight success on left. Our casualties 108 wounded. Very little hostile artillery fire in reply to our barrage.	Mottt Capt & adjt
"	31/12/17		Quiet day. Casualties nil. Work continued during the night on posts wire	Mottt Capt & adjt Mottt Capt & adjt Lt-Col Commanding 2/4 Bolton Regt

WAR DIARY
or
INTELLIGENCE SUMMARY

(Erase heading not required.)

Army Form C. 2118.

SECRET

War Diary
2/11th London Regt.

From 1st Jan 1918
To 31st Jan 1918

Vol 13

Army Form C. 2118.

WAR DIARY
or
INTELLIGENCE SUMMARY.
(Erase heading not required.)

80(2/11 Bonder Regt.

Place	Date	Hour	Summary of Events and Information	Remarks and references to Appendices
LEFT SUB SECTOR TELEGRAPHE	1/1/18	10pm	Quiet day. Batt. relieved in the line by 2/5 Ldn Regt. Relief complete 8.30pm. Nil casualties. Batt. on relief proceeded to BATTLE entrained for READING, then marched to BRIDGE CAMP	
BRIDGE CAMP	2/1/18		Day spent in resting, cleaning up.	
"	3/1/18		Extract from Lon Gaz dated 1/1/18 Lt Col Lynmode awarded D.S.O. Lt Col Lynmode & not known Lt Col Stafford 11/1/18 M.I.D Lt Qr.Mr & Hon.Lieut J W Jackson Do	Capt Copy Capt
"	4/1/18		Brigadier's Inspection & Parades for Presentation of awards by Corps Commander. Extracts Lond Gazette 4/1/18 Capt & Major Hunt awarded MC	Capt
"	5/1/18		Xmas festivities during the day. Xmas dinner	Copy Capt
"	6/1/18		Day of Prayer & Thanksgiving appointed by the King. Church service in C.A. Huts. Lt Col.	Copy Capt
"	7/1/18	7.55 AM	Batt. moved from BRIDGE CAMP to HOUTKERQUE AREA E 26 a 74 (34 a 2)	Copy Capt

Army Form C. 2118.

WAR DIARY
or
INTELLIGENCE SUMMARY (81) 2/n London Regt b

(Erase heading not required.)

Instructions regarding War Diaries and Intelligence Summaries are contained in F. S. Regs., Part II. and the Staff Manual respectively. Title Pages will be prepared in manuscript.

Place	Date	Hour	Summary of Events and Information	Remarks and references to Appendices
HOUTKER QUE AREA E.26.d.94.	7/1/18		Bn. over road, entraining at EVERDINGHE STATION @ 9 am proceeding to PROVEN, thence light Railway to E.16.d.2d & marching to E.26.d.94.	Capt & adjt
"	8/1/18	10am	Company Training	Capt & adjt
"	9/1/18	"	do.	Capt & adjt
"	10/1/18	"	Brigade Inspection on Brigade Parade ground at E.20.b.3y	Capt & adjt
"	11/1/18	"	Battn. firing on Ranges E.25.A.4.4.4. Practices 10 new nature 8 & 5 new subsection. All guns turns fired.	Capt & adjt
"	12/1/18	"	Brigade Parade at E.20.b.3.y for inspection & presentation of Ribands by 2nd Corps Commander. Officers French Church Army Hut. HOUTKERQUE	Capt & adjt
"	13/1/18	"		Capt & adjt
"	14/1/18	"	Bathing Company Training	Capt & adjt

2449 Wt. W14957/M90 750,000 1/16 J.B.C. & A. Forms/C.2118/12.

WAR DIARY
or
INTELLIGENCE SUMMARY

Army Form C. 2118.

(82) 2/4 Lon Regt.

Place	Date	Hour	Summary of Events and Information	Remarks and references to Appendices
HOUTKERQUE AREA E26.d.4.4	15/1/18	5pm	Company training	Watts Capt actg
"	16/1/18		Company training	Watts Capt actg
"	17/1/18		Company training. Tactical exercises for officers.	Watts Capt actg
"	18/1/18		Battn route march. Route:- Watou. Houtkerque, Drogland, Winnezeele	Watts Capt a/c
"	19/1/18		Company training. Firing on Range. B Coy → 35 ORs AQ moved to Northern Camp, Proven to act as Brigade loading party during move.	Watts Capt a/c
"	20/1/18	10:40 AM	Battn moved from Houtkerque area to Central Camp, using tents before entraining at Proven Stn at 3.30 AM on 21/1/18. Entrained 24 offs. 401 ORs. 66 horses. 40 axles for Villers Bretonneux at 3.30am & detrained at 3.30pm	Watts Capt a/c
"	21/1/18			

Army Form C. 2118.

WAR DIARY
or
INTELLIGENCE SUMMARY
(Erase heading not required.)

(P3) 2/11 London Regt=

Place	Date	Hour	Summary of Events and Information	Remarks and references to Appendices
GUISY & BLANGY.	22/1/18	-	Thence marched to GUISY & BLANGY-TRONVILLE. AHd HQ to GUISY. C+D to BLANGY. Arrived in billets at 8.30 pm	
"	23/1/18	10am	Day spent in cleaning up. Company training classes	
"	24/1/18	"	- Do - 8 classes	
"	25/1/18	"	- Do - 8 classes & no firing in range	
"	26/1/18	"	- Do - do -	
"	27/1/18	"	Bathing. Orders received that Battn was to be disbanded under AG's Authorities 164/4 (O) AAG 58 Army No. 2460/5. 58th Divn AS/4/140 58th Divn 15/404 G.HQ 3rd Echelon letter 5/404 dated 11/8. Postings as use as follows: 10 officers 350 ORs to be transferred to 1/20 London Regt. 1 officer 200 ORs to be transferred	

WAR DIARY or INTELLIGENCE SUMMARY

Army Form C. 2118.

(84) 2/16th London Regt.

Place	Date	Hour	Summary of Events and Information	Remarks and references to Appendices
GUISY BERGAY	27/1/18		8 Officers & 280 ORs to the 1/22nd London Regt.	
"	28/1/18	11am	Church Service. Bathing.	
"	29/1/18		Day spent in preparation for disbandment.	
"	30/1/18	6am	All ranks for transfer paraded Barney Square & entered buses. The following officers & men proceeded to the 4 Pdn Div. at BERTINCOURT:— 2Lt S. Claydon, Capt W.J. Lowe M.C., 2Lt N. Flynn M.C., Maj W. Warren M.C., 2Lt S.M. Rood, 2Lt W.M. Logan, 2Lt W.J. Warren, 2Lt A.B. Yorke & 350 ORs. 2Lt H. Morton, Capt W.R. Wood, 2Lt In. Hannay, 2Lt J.A. Young, 2Lt E. Parkinson, 2Lt H.C. Gill, 2Lt E.Y. Underhill — 195 ORs to 1/5 London Regt. 2Lt Y.J. Young, 2Lt H.C. Gill, 2Lt C.Y. Underhill, N.C. 58 Bn Son. Att. 1/2nd Scot Rifles, 2Lt L.J. Dudley & Lt W. Spence at R.D. Anderson & 2Lt G.A. Boyer, 2Lt V.S. Green, 2Lt ... Ambridge to 1 R.W. Fus. Lt R.W. Morris & 240 ORs.	
"	31/1/18		Balance of 159 OR consisting of 80 Sergeants & 71 ORs. Major Y. P. Lewis Day Caps vary of Frobr. 2/Lt P.H. Halliday 70 & 66 ORs remaining at GUISY to complete disbandment.	

N. Lewiston
MAJOR COMMANDING